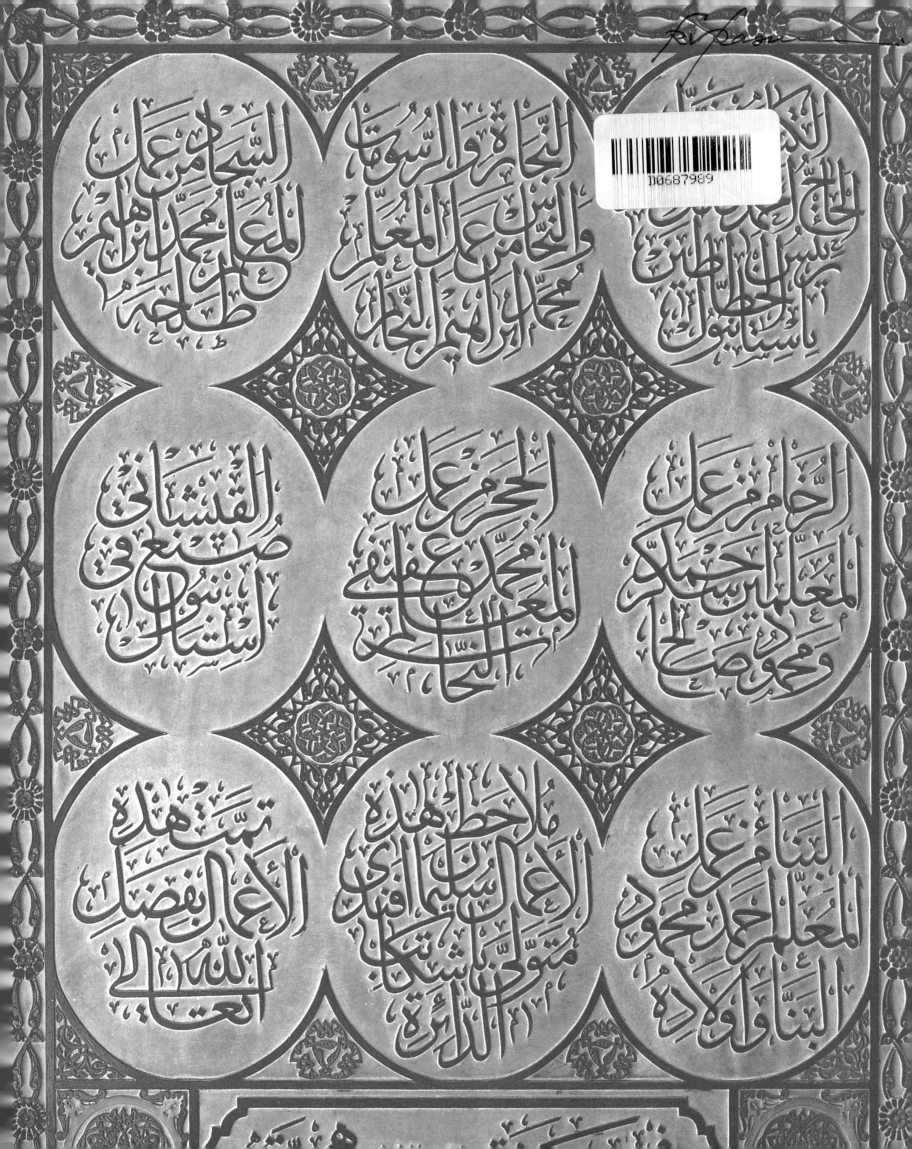

EGYPTIAN PALACES AND VILLAS

PASHAS, KHEDIVES, AND KINGS

SHIRLEY JOHNSTON with Sherif Sonbol

ABRAMS, NEW YORK

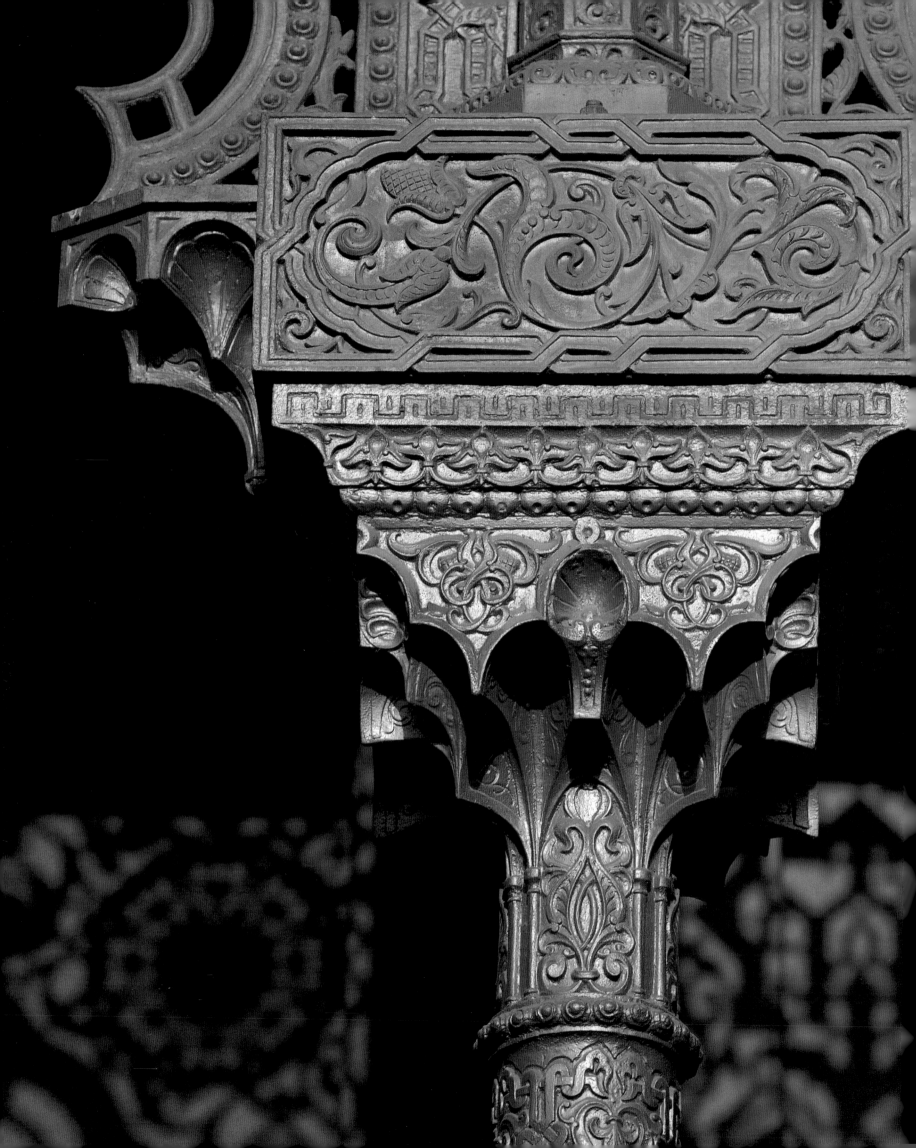

TABLE OF CONTENTS

ACKNOWLEDGMENTS

PAGE 1
This Napoleonic marble eagle commissioned by the Khedive Ismail for the redecoration of his Gezira Island palace today is the symbol of modern Egypt.

PAGES 2–3
The deceptively plain building of the Cataract Hotel on its rocky cliff above the Nile at Aswan belies the comfort and luxury inside. World celebrities continue to frequent the hotel where Agatha Christie worked on writing *Death on the Nile*.

PAGE 4
A cast-iron column capital at the Gezira Palace. Architect Carl von Diebitsch first tested his technique on a colossal zinc vase etched with Islamic decorations for the World's Fair of 1862 in London.

OPPOSITE
The great stained-glass ceiling at Zaafaran Palace illuminates a central stairwell recalling that of the Casino at Baden-Baden.

I expected Egypt to be fast and easy. The people are nice, and the weather is good. I thought I would even have time to spare. I could sail up the Nile and go to the beach. After all, my book was to be about Egypt and the splendors of its recent past, the nineteenth century and six decades of the twentieth. Next to the pharaohs, this would be a snap, so I imagined.

How wrong I was! For I discovered an Egypt as rich and colorful and exciting as its ancient past! Forget that people said much had been lost or destroyed. The more I explored, the more I found that amazing forgotten treasures lay behind the dusty facades of cities and towns and villages—stretching from the Delta to the Nile Valley down south. There was so much to see, so much to learn. Where to begin? Where to end? No one back home would believe this! I felt like a Belzoni, a Champollion, even Howard Carter. And today I can still turn a corner and be taken aback by yet another simple incredible gem. Who would have ever expected all of this?

I spent five continuous years in Egypt for this book, and am consoled by a popular local saying that *fi Masr kulla haaga mumkin*, "in Egypt everything is possible." For indeed it is. Five years have passed and now I am looking to find the nearest beach!

This book is not a nostalgic interlude. This book is about life. I have dramatized Egypt and its places, people, and events, relying on the scholarly works of many authors in many languages. I also have drawn from the stories and tales that Egyptian families have passed along from one to another for generations. I've tried to separate fact from fiction to re-create in the words of architect Ahmad Hamid, "the teenage or adolescent story of modern life in Egypt through a cosmopolitan multi-layering of times, epochs, hours, years, people, all that has become the warp and weft of a thick jacquard culture of life . . . These could be settings for dramas, passionate operettas, or conspiratorial detective plots, even in Cairo, mannerist Victorian sensualities."

I am indebted to many people, among them Samir Rafaat and his nearly encyclopedic writings about the people and places of modern Egypt. He is to be admired as a pioneer, as should also be the art historian and architect Mercédès Volait in Paris. Others, both in Egypt and abroad, also are producing great works, and they too are to be commended.

For my transliterations of the Arabic into English, I've taken the advice of T. E. Lawrence, who once said the best tack was to come out of the desert leaving the Arabic dictionary behind. In a word, anything goes. If the Chennaoui family prefers the French spelling of their name, as opposed to the English spelling, "Shinnawi," so be it. Reminding me about Lawrence was my friend Raymond Stock, an Arabist and a scholar, to whom I am especially thankful for sharing with me his vast and deep knowledge.

Photography came to Egypt soon after its invention. And Egyptians have always been keen on taking pictures. But in recent years, photography has fallen out of the mainstream. People have forgotten that it is a true form of art. To the families who kindly allowed photography of their residences for this book—many of them with names that are still famous throughout the Middle East—I thank each of you very much.

I am grateful to Mohamed Hassouna for his advice and support, and to Vincenzo Nesci for his continued enthusiasm for this project from the start.

I also want to extend my gratitude to culture minister Farouk Hosni, Dr. Gaballa Ali Gaballa, former head of the Supreme Council of Antiquities, and Dr. Ahmed Nawar, president of the National Center for Fine Arts, for allowing several palaces under their purview to appear in this book. I thank Salah Shakweer for the Monasterly Salamlik, Dr. Youssef Wali and his family, and in the provinces the governors Hassan Hemaida of Minya, and Mohamed Sayed Swan of Dakahliya. And I thank His Excellency François Dopffer, former ambassador of France in Egypt, for permission to photograph his residence and chancellery, as well as for theirs, the ambassadors of the United Kingdom, Italy, Turkey, Mexico, and the Vatican.

I also am grateful to the Accor Hotel group in Egypt for allowing photography of the Winter Palace and the Cataract; the Marriott organization for Gezira Palace; the El-Salamlik Palace and Hotel in Alexandria for its Montaza establishment; and the Oberoi hotel chain for Mena House at the pyramids. I am indebted to the Desert Research Institute just outside of Cairo for permitting pictures of the former Youssef Kamal residence, and the Rectorate of Ain Shams University for allowing us to photograph the former Zaafaran Palace that is now its offices.

Special thanks also is extended to Youssef Mansour and his family, and Nejla Maghrabi for her help, as well as to Turkish Ambassador Korkmaz Haktanir and his wife Handan, Belgian Ambassador Guy Trouveroy and his wife Nathalie, as well as my friend Mrs. Poonam Ayoub, and her husband Arif, the ambassador of Pakistan in Cairo. I also want to thank former American deputy chief of mission Reno Harnish and his wife Leslie.

In Paris, helping to launch this book early on were author Gilbert Sinoué, Nadia Sednaoui, Evi Larsen, Daniel de Lamaze, Prince Aziz Toussoun, Robin Tait, Jean Martin, and, in Monaco, Mark Armstrong of Sotheby's.

In Cairo and Alexandria, I want to thank Bridget McKinney, Jacqueline Younes, Mehri Foda and Joyce Reeves Foda (for also showing me their family's great old palace in Kafr Tamboul in the Delta where "we still use mosquito nets"), Mediha and Prince Abbas Hilmi, Said Zulficar, Selim Sednaoui, Nadia Lamlum, Mona Abaza Radwan, Josey Wahbah, the late Saad Abd el-Nour, Baghat Badawy, the Mohamed Kamels in Dokki; as well as George Kypreos, Lussette de Saab, Nadim Zaidan (for his memories of Maadi), Mohamed Awad, Carolyn Gaultier, Dr. Hasan Khalil, Mamdouh El-Meniawy, Neville Youssri, Miguelle Yansouni; and Margot Badran, Lorenzo Montesini, Lois Crooks, Vivian Campbell, Zeinab Hassouna, Hussein Fakhry, Patrick Werr, interior decorator Ihab Shafik, Mahmoud Sabit, Mohamed Shawki, Naguib Abdallah, Sabil and Teddy Maggar, Samira Megally, Mona Korashy, Samia Sonbol, as well as the dean of Cairo's school of fine arts, Mohamed Tawfik Abdel Gawaad, and journalist Moguib Rushdi.

In the Delta, I am also grateful to Mickey Khalil and his family in Mehalla el-Kubra, and the Ibrahim family near Kafr el-Sheikh; and in Assiout, the Tammams of Saleh Salem. I also am grateful to the late Mustapha Zeinaty for his kind permission to photograph his house in Armant.

I have made the libraries of the American University in Cairo my second home, and at the Rare Books Library, I appreciate the help of assistant director Daad Abd el-Razik. I also thank the French institutes IFAO and CEDEJ in Cairo for allowing me to use their research facilities, and, at the Egyptian Geographic Society, the director William B. Nessim, the staff of the Islamic Museum; and, in Alexandria, the staff of the Institute of Archaeology, the Greek consulate and former consul-general Michael Daratzikis, and librarian and archivist Aleco Vlahos, as well as Vassilis Filippatos, director of the Foundation for Hellenic Culture.

I also appreciate the efforts on my behalf by Dr. Wolfgang Koehler, Rudolf Agnster of the Austrian foreign office in Vienna, Dr. István Ormos in Budapest, the Instituto Italiano in Cairo, Volker Harms-Ziegler of the Institut für Stadtgeschichte,

The Toussoun Abu Gabal house at Giza was built of reinforced concrete, but with niches, restrained *muqarnas*, *mashrabiya* windows, and a barrel-vault dome invisible from the street. Here the architect Hassan Fathy was "playing with memory."

Frankfurt, Isolde Lehnert, librarian of the German Archaeological Institute in Cairo, Dr. Cornelius von Pilgrim, director in Cairo of the Swiss Institute of Architectural and Archaeological Research on Ancient Egypt, the embassy of the Netherlands, and, in London, Dr. Mariam Rosser-Owen at the Victoria and Albert Museum, the staff of the Royal Institute of British Architects, Harold Beaton, author Trevor Mostyn; as well as Angela Cipriani in Rome at the Academy of San Luca, Eric Egan in Milan, Marlis Scarry in Geneva, H. J. Badrutt in Zurich, Cathy Ni Cheallaigh of the mayor's office in Roermond, Holland (for architect Leon Stienon), and John Ambrose at Fragments of Time in Boston.

I am also grateful for the support of my parents in Delaware, and thank the state's U.S. senator Joseph Biden for his efforts on my behalf with the Egyptian presidency. My cousin Susan Jackewicz in Florida is also to be lauded for seeking out information when I reached a brick wall here.

At Harry N. Abrams, I am most grateful to Eric Himmel, editor in chief, for his enthusiastic support of the book; to Elaine Stainton, my editor, for her many thoughtful suggestions; to Darilyn Carnes, for her extraordinarily beautiful design; and to Jane G. Searle, who oversaw the book's production with a meticulous hand and eye.

My thanks also goes to Peter Snowdon in Brussels for his thoughtful comments on the narrative.

Lastly, I could not have done this book without photographer Sherif Sonbol. He stuck it out with me on this project for the long five years, which alone is a major accomplishment. I thank the *Al-Ahram Weekly* organization, the late Hosni Guindy, and chief editor Hani Shukrallah, for giving him time off to work with me. And a great bravo also goes to Antar Photo Stores in Cairo.

Shirley Johnston
Heliopolis
24 June 2005

INTRODUCTION

Not long ago, Egyptian state television presented a serial about Cairo's good old days in the 1910s, *The Age of Emad el-Din Street*. Emad el-Din was a swank yet popular hangout for artists and musicians, lined with theatres, cabarets, and coffee houses, where everyone from the hoi polloi to the *beau monde* came to listen to Sayed Darwish, the talented young singer and *oud* player still cherished by Egyptians to this day. Only a few years earlier, the sandy street had offered little hint of its future, save for one lone European "palace" and its wooden-paneled Club of the Princes.

Everything had changed dramatically once Ernesto di Farro began working on the Aswan dam at the turn of the century. For this specialist in concrete with offices in London and businesses throughout the Middle East had brought with him a new system of constructing buildings with multiple stories on unstable ground—no small consideration in Egypt. Suddenly, Cairo was growing up, and by 1911, Emad el-Din Street boasted a city landmark: a pair of Edwardian apartment buildings resembling the Hotel Negresco in Nice!

So enthusiastic about his new buildings on Emad el-Din Street was the ruling khedive, Abbas Hilmi II, still a young man in his thirties, that he inspected the works nearly every day, climbing up scaffolding, negotiating deep canyons, and walking over wobbly planks with confidence. For these Khedivial Buildings represented a second coming of the Belle Epoque for Abbas Hilmi and his architect, Antonio Lasciac.

Abbas Hilmi's grandfather, the Khedive Ismail, had been the builder of modern Cairo. A cotton boom in the early 1860s had allowed him to realize some of the lofty dreams of his own grandfather, the ambitious Mohamed Ali Pasha. Rising to power after Napoleon Bonaparte's short-lived conquest of Egypt, this impressive character of oriental cunning and vigor, an Albanian from Cavalla in Northern Greece, had come to rule Ottoman Egypt as its pasha in 1805, paying the sultan an annual tribute for a *pashalik* that reached as far as the Sudan. Building up his independent power to make himself and his descendants effective lords of the land, Mohamed Ali at one point controlled Arabia, Crete, and Syria. The dynasty he founded would endure until the abdication of his great-great grandson, King Farouk, in 1952.

Ismail had envisioned himself as the "Emperor of Africa," gatekeeper of the main route to India and the East. Nevertheless, Europe was most often on his mind after he had been sent by his grandfather to France at age fourteen on a "scholarly mission." That sojourn had left a lasting impression. A later trip in 1867 to the Exposition Universelle in the Paris of Haussman would trigger Ismail's self-proclaimed "mania for building." The result was, in the words of architect Mohamed Awad, director of the AlexMed research center at the Biblioteca Alexandrina, "the first boom of many booms."

The Khedive Ismail not only rushed into massive public works and urban development to create a grand Cairo beyond the limits of the old Fatimid, Mameluke, and Ottoman cities. He also initiated far-reaching industrial and agricultural projects:

The mosque at Manial Palace dating to 1933 resembles a sanctuary in the Muqattam hills above Cairo erected by the Fatimid vizier and builder of Armenian origin, Badr al-Gamali. Seven tiled panels display the work of Istanbul's chief of calligraphers, Ahmed Kamil Effendi, known for suspending large, dramatic writing on walls in *al-maraya* style—that is, in mirror-image script—to create a pleasing artistic effect.

railroads, roads, and telegraph lines; postal services; barrages and canals; and schools. And with these came a pressing need for palaces. For Ismail was the last Egyptian ruler to keep a harem! And his ladies needed both winter and summer palaces—with columned verandas and loggias, and open patios, not to mention parks and gardens with kiosks, and pathways and ponds and streams, and bridges and grottoes and waterfalls. The ladies had more utilitarian needs, too, for stables, kitchens, and other dependencies. Palaces also were necessary for the soirées and spectacles to honor the foreign elites attending the stellar event of the nineteenth century—Ismail's gala opening of the Suez Canal in 1869. And the palaces worked: "I've never seen anything like it in my life," the visiting Empress Eugénie wrote to her husband, Napoleon III, in France.

A steady stream of architects, painters, decorators and furniture makers from the northern rim of the Mediterranean responded to the call of the grand master of Ottoman hospitality and display. Coming mostly from the academies of Italy, the new arrivals edged out Mohamed Ali's old *Rumi* artists and artisans from European Turkey, the Aegean islands, coastal Asia Minor, and the Balkans.

No doubt the task of housing the Khedive Ismail and his fourteen wives and children was still best met by a Turkish *saray*—a residential complex with separate quarters for men to receive guests, called a *salamlik*, and another for the family, known as the *haramlik*, literally, the "forbidden area." Like their compatriots working in Istanbul, the European architects and craftsmen brought to Egypt their neoclassical ideas along with Carrara marble for staircases and fireplaces—winter nights even in Africa could be cold—and salons of French marquetry, canapés, and side chairs.

But was this really Egypt? Suddenly Cairo had the latest from Paris. Keyhole arches were *à la mode*, as were wooden geometric inlays for ceilings and doors, stalactite soffits, arabesque cornices, marble mosaics, and ceramic tiles. The talent behind this renewed oriental effervescence was an Italian craftsman, Giuseppe Parvis. From his Cairo ateliers, he could transform wood, ivory, mother of pearl, copper, bronze, silver, and gold into superb credenzas and buffets, chairs, and precious coffers! The forgotten arts of the pharaohs, the Ptolemies, the caliphs, and Mamelukes gave way to a gloriously modern revival. "This man alone is a Renaissance in himself!" marveled the early-twentieth-century historian L. A. Balboni. For Parvis—engraver, bronzesmith, sculptor, cabinetmaker, and decorator in styles ranging from Islamic and Egyptian through Pompeian to Rinascimento, and even Japanese—was working not only for Ismail, but for all the big new pashas and the foreign owners of the even bigger new hotels. It was no surprise to find Parvis winning a gold medal at the Paris Exposition of 1867—followed by honors in Milan, Vienna, Antwerp, Amsterdam, his hometown Turin, and Philadelphia.

Parvis and his sons, along with the brothers Jacovelli from Bari, would also produce "a wide variety of furniture in the *style arabe* which every palace or edifice of prestige had to have in its salons," as French architect and art historian Mercédès Volait has observed. Even Lord Cromer—at the helm once the British had arrived to provide "protection" to Egypt—had sought out the Jacovellis to redecorate his consulate for the benefit of a touring Prince of Wales. The same Jacovellis would also add their magic to the Club of the Princes on Emad el-Din Street.

Enormous inlaid oriental chests signed GP still line the long and wide corridors of Ismail's palace on the Nile island of Gezira. Modeled on the Alhambra, the palace was designed by another Vienna Polytechnic graduate and Egypt's chief for the preservation of Arab monuments, the German architect Julius Franz. The Moorish cast-iron verandas created by Berlin's Carl von Diebitsch also are still there, although changed with time. According to Nisha Sursock, the descendant of a later owner, "they used to be green, the color of the iron, not this fake gold."

Some of Ismail's "palaces" in truth were hasty, lath-and-plaster Potemkin constructions which have since disappeared wholly or in part. Ismail's son and successor, Tewfik, decided not to move into the Gezira *saray* after his court architect Fabricius Pasha discovered just how bad its foundations were. The same Fabricius later pulled down all but two of these buildings to make way for a luxury establishment for its new Swiss owners, the Baehler hotel group. Today, the palace is managed by the Marriott organization.

In the end, Ismail would abdicate his throne. But before he stepped down, he had totally transformed Egypt and its architectural culture. "Ever since then, the Egyptians have been curious about Europeans, and have spent a century and half exploring this curiosity," observes Professor Awad, himself belonging to a family of Alexandrian builders. His words echo those of historian Robert Ilbert on the pre-1920s period, when "European eclecticism reigned as master." The "preponderance of *italianisante*," which, Ilbert notes, was naturally visible in Alexandria, where the taxi cabs still are Fiats. This penchant for things Italian was expressed by "a very marked sumptuous taste, especially in the grand residences of the local bourgeoisie and in the buildings of great companies and banks." For this clientele "was particularly sensitive to the effects of fashion, being European less by origin than as a manner of living."

This "golden age" that gave us Emad el-Din Street with its carnival of façades in plaster, stucco, and marble, was also an age of grand millionaires who easily outmatched even the new industrialists in France! And their euphoria segued into the interwar period, which was, to quote Professor Awad again, "the biggest boom of all." The houses of the interwar period represented, for Ilbert, the "first great modern works." As such, they reflected a "remarkable rupture" with the heavy decorative style of the past. This was also a period of radical innovation: in 1927 the new methods and tastes derived from the French *système Hennebique*, or ferro-concrete construction, allowed Gustave Perret, the designer of the Théâtre des Champs-Élysées in Paris, to design an Alexandrian house for his fellow architect Gustave Aghion in simple, but beautiful, raw concrete.

And where did the *style arabe* go? "Many of these villas and houses were destroyed to give place to grand apartment buildings," Ilbert writes. "But the style remained essential for grand public buildings until the thirties." Today, we can only see in old black-and-white photos the exquisite oriental ornamentation of the neo-Mameluke house in Ismailia designed for Count Antoine de Zogheb at the turn of the century by architect Herz Bey, a product of the Vienna Polytechnic, successor to Franz Pasha as Arab monuments chief, and director of the national museum of Arab art. The developer who bought the house pulled it down only to find that the ground would not support his planned high-rise. The spot now is a large parking lot.

My purpose in this book is not to lament the losses of the past. For there are many gems that still exist today: treasures such as the Manial Palace of Prince Mohamed Ali Tewfik, dedicated to the arts of Islam, and now a museum. There also is the lasting presence of the Belgian industrialist Baron Empain and his "city of the sun," Heliopolis, designed in Brussels to a European plan, but ornamented to resemble the thousand-nights fantasy of some oriental sultan. Not to be forgotten is the native son Hassan Fathy and his modern Islamic house on the banks of the Nile in Giza.

There are also many traces of Ilbert's "total eclecticism," which integrated the European plan with all the traditional decorations of Islamic art. We can see it in Abbas Hilmi's court architect Antonio Lasciac's Tuscan hall for Prince Youssef Kamal with its tiled oriental salons, and even in Minya, where a Bedouin chief built a house with salons by the Jacovellis! Today's Egyptians are as curious about Europeans as their forbears. You can see the evidence everywhere. Gated communities with sprawling Mediterranean villas, swimming pools, and gardens have sprung up around golf clubs in the sandy desert near Alexandria, while beyond the "St. Tropez" that once was Agami, with its watch-towers and fig trees by the sea, there is now talk of creating a new Egyptian Riviera. Springing up all around Cairo are new satellites, which have both the old and the new guard thinking about moving out of exclusive Zamalek, Giza, and Garden City, to reverse a trend set in motion fifty years ago when Nasser's revolution brought everyone into the cities from the provinces.

Indeed, it is hard to keep track of so many comings and goings. One day *Al-Ahram Hebdo* shouts in French: "Bad taste reigns everywhere"; the next, the *Egyptian Gazette*, has its two cents in bold-type English: "Egypt lacks architectural unity." In the words of Professor Awad, Egypt is suffering from "not a clash, but a crash of civilizations."

One episode of *Emad el-Din Street* tells the story of a fellah from the countryside who joins his colleagues for his first look inside a "modern" palace. For these peasant fellaheen, nothing has changed since the days of the pharaohs. Since time immemorial the mud-plastered *mastaba* or step-bench, has been their seat. But on Emad el-Din Street they discover, to their amazement, a suite of French canapés and side chairs. "Look at that," says one to another in tones of wonder: "It's a *mastaba*."

The humor was well intended. Yet it should be pointed out that for centuries Egypt's rulers had sat cross-legged on fringed floor cushions or broad Ottoman divans under dim lights. The move into brilliantly lit salons with sofas and chairs of all the Louis—Louis XIV, Louis XV, and Louis XVI, even Louis XIII—came late and suddenly, even if it appeared to be definitive. Indeed it took the French, in the 1920s, to bring the divan back into fashion in the form of the Art Deco *chaise longue!*

But there is no such thing as going backwards in Egypt. For *tous les Louis* had come to stay, and would only be replaced by "Louis Farouk," the gaudy taste of the country's last king. Today one can find these gilded monstrosities "in every house and at every level of society," notes Lois Crooks, a long-time Cairo resident and collector of oriental furniture: "even—can you believe it?—lining the walls, just like the old divans!"

The TV comedy continued as the fellaheen were confronted with a chandelier armed with light bulbs shaped like flames. "What is that?" they mused. And the response came: "A candle packed in glass!" While everyone needs to laugh at themselves now and then, apparently the writers had forgotten that such lamps were as old as Egypt, and that the Arabs had copied glass lamps from Coptic ecclesiastics—early Christians who, they said, descended from the pharaohs.

Soon after the program was broadcast, a top government advisor started thinking out loud about how the palaces of the last centuries might be preserved. After all, where could the art of building hope to be taken seriously if not in Egypt, home to the first of all builders, the pharaohs? Was not the pharaoh, literally, *per aa*, "the Great House"?

To measure the distance that official thinking has come, one has only to remember the comments made by Frank Lloyd Wright during a visit to Cairo in June 1957. He had stopped by to see some of his former students. And he was not pleased by what he saw:

"You, gentlemen, you the engineers have been responsible. What I have seen is absolutely blank, the present constructions are lacking of all soul, all life, with no respect, no pride accorded to man and that which is human. . . . I am being honest with you. . . . In all your works I have not seen any cooperation between the architect and the engineer . . . This proves that you have conceived these works using only your head in applying the rules and theories of the universities but without putting in the heart. Science alone does not suffice, gentlemen."

I came to Egypt, looking for what Wright called the "heart" and "soul" that makes good architecture. Wright would be happy to know that I found much that he evidently did not see. From Alexandria to Aswan, there are palaces, villas, and houses imbued with his kind of heart and soul. Many are preserved as residences of foreign ambassadors, dignitaries, and other diplomats; others have been turned into international institutions; a few are hotels. Others are private. Yet many, if not all, are surprising.

Who would have expected to come upon an Andalusian creation rising to the sublime on the banks of the Nile in Sohag? Who would have thought that Girga would be home to a proud riverside Victorian mansion? Or that Ismail's resthouse in Armant might make us dream of sugar?

There is no space in this book to discuss every significant building, or even every major builder, in this great land. Instead, I hope I can give you an idea of what Wright was talking about when he told his former students to "put in the sentiments, make the heart vibrate with emotion, and let these become the electromotive force of any work." This is what I have tried to capture in telling the "stories" of these splendid residences, and of their architects, builders, decorators, and owners.

Nearly everything in the Golden Hall of Prince Mohamed Ali Tewfik's Manial Palace is of gilt-work, including the "forest" of columns shaped like palm trees. The entire room, which had belonged to the prince's maternal grandfather, Ilhami Pasha, was shipped to Cairo from Istanbul. Surmounting the entrance door, within a sunburst, is the prince's *tughra*, or imperial Ottoman monogram.

A love of gardening inspired Pince Mohamed Ali Tewfik to decorate this room of his Manial Palace with floral Turkish tiles. The furniture dates to the 1930s.

GAWHARA PALACE

The Citadel, Cairo. 1812–14; rebuilt thereafter

A s the new viceroy of Egypt, ruling in the name of the Ottoman Turkish sultan, Mohamed Ali Pasha, could not rest easy nights. Enormous power and wealth awaited him. But what had he done to achieve this position? He had destroyed his rivals, the last of the Mameluke beys, or princes, whose families had ruled Egypt for centuries. Only a year earlier, he had invited some forty of these princes to Cairo's citadel for a magnificent dinner—and to certain death. Now his massacre of the Mamelukes had begun to worry him. What if their ghosts were haunting the citadel?

Mohamed Ali quickly decided what to do. He would demolish the ancient palaces of their forbears, the sultans Qaitbay and Al-Ghouri, and build a palace of his own. Like most newcomers to power, Mohamed Ali also wanted to leave his own stamp on the walled stronghold where Egypt's conquerors had lived and reigned for seven centuries before him. Encouraged each year by the imperial Ottoman *firman* confirming him as Pasha of Egypt, he began to renew the massive fortress built by the great Saladin back in 1183. Doubtless El-Aziz, "the high and precious one," as he was called, also was concerned about his personal safety. His former residence had been sacked by his own Albanian guards for lack of pay.

To rebuild and refit the citadel to withstand modern cannon and muskets, Mohamed Ali brought in a team of *Rumi*— that is, European—artisans: Greeks, Turks, Bulgarians, and Albanians. They would erect barracks, schools, an arsenal, a gun-powder factory, and a mint. But above all, they gave the pasha a palace to equal those of Constantinople—a rambling two-story pavilion, a Turkish *kushk*. The palace called *gawhara*, or "jewel," had rectangular Western windows, often topped by an oval *oeil-de-boeuf*, which seemed to relegate to the oriental past the use of *mashrabiyas*, or turned-wood screens; the Pasha also had banned them for failing to keep out the heat and dust. Yet nothing appeared more Ottoman than undulating semicircular hoods above Palladian-style porticoes, while Byzantine ideas resurfaced in small wooden cupolas studded with octagonal cabochons in blue and gold.

The French engineer and architect Pascal Coste also was brought in to add quarters for functionaries and servants. The result was a practical combination of residential and working spaces, with a *haush*, or courtyard, on one side, and on the other, high above the ramparts, wide-open views toward the Nile and the Great Pyramids.

Were the Mamelukes seeking revenge? Suddenly the pasha's second son died from the plague at his home in Rosetta. Then, in June 1820, a two-day fire destroyed the palace's wooden construction and painted interiors. Not to be discouraged, Mohamed Ali installed a large marble fountain, columned stone terraces and porticoes, parterres of flower beds and orange groves, and even a menagerie containing a lion, two tigers, and an elephant, a gift of British Lord Hastings. Sadly, a hippopotamus, a symbol of protection in the land of the pharaohs, died of sunstroke.

Were the Mamelukes not yet satisfied? Mohamed Ali's third son was captured and burnt alive by the natives in the Sudan

Courted by Western powers as the gatekeeper to the East, the Ottoman *wali*, or governor, Mohamed Ali Pasha, received many official gifts, among them an ebony secretary made in Italy and inlaid with ivory in the Pompeian style. Shown here is a detail of the inlay.

The raised platform at the far end of an upper-floor reception hall showcases a monumental gilt "Throne of Egypt," designed in Rome to accommodate Mohamed Ali Pasha, who preferred sitting in the oriental manner. The lions on the chair's armrests represent courage—a necessity for a pasha who had ended five hundred and fifty years of Mameluke rule in Egypt. The crown at the top was added a century later.

in 1822. And less than two years later, in March 1824, the palace once again was struck by fire, sparked by explosions of gunpowder. The pasha rebuilt anew, bringing in enormous slabs of Italian marble for a vestibule, a massive staircase, and wide airy corridors; eighteen-foot squares were laid down for flooring. Ottoman meagerness indeed had given way to opulence, befitting a Pasha of Egypt.

By 1825, English visitor Anne Catherine Elwood, noted "the grand room could offer dancing, had deep niches for conversation, and side-rooms for music, reading, games, and refreshments." Its lofty walls, however, featured wide cornices painted with Turkish landscapes that lacked any understanding of the rules of perspective. Yet few were looking upward when at eye level were brightly colored floor-cushions, cashmere shawls edged in gold fringe, superb carpets from Persia and Turkey alongside others sent as gifts from England. "One also could see a little bit everywhere the simple ornament of a crescent, accompanied by one star, which is the sign of the Ottoman power," Mrs. Elwood noted.

As time passed, the palace grew ever more splendid. The divans once covered in gold and silver brocades were redone in *gorge de pigeon* satin with long blue fringe. Huge stained-glass windows lined entire rooms; and walls were covered in green and purple velour with repeating motifs of tulips and roses. This was "one of the most beautiful edifices of the Muslim empire," noted one British visitor, although a compatriot thought the palace "infinitely less beautiful and less spacious than Shoubra." The English civil engineer Galloway Bey, meanwhile, was more impressed by the fact that the men working for him on the pasha's gas lighting system had told him there was enough space "to receive eight hundred women."

By 1848, a French traveler observed that the palace was furnished "sumptuously, in a style much more Louis XIV than Moorish." Yet in spite of its rich furnishings *à l'européenne*, the building remained an oriental labyrinth, built from its owner's fears and fantasies. As another visitor put it: "This was a simple and severe construction, hiding under the eyes a fortress within a fortress . . . that masked, in many ways, a thousand detours."

Did Mohamed Ali Pasha add European windows to his new palace behind the citadel walls in order to better see the Nile and the Great Pyramids? Or was he looking out for his enemies?

Originally an empty hall, save for oriental sofas around its walls, Mohamed Ali's official divan, or audience chamber, still contains the one-thousand-kilogram chandelier sent to him by Louis-Philippe of France. Mohamed Ali's portrait on the far wall replicates the much-copied work of English painter Thomas Bridgestocke, who had visited Egypt in 1847. The pasha's appearance in many journals and reviews made him a well-recognized figure abroad, especially in France, where many copies of his portrait were made by Vernet, one dedicated to Vivant-Denon.

SHOUBRA PALACE: NYMPHAEUM

Shoubra. 1808–21

Spring ws in the air, the roses in bloom, and exciting news swept through Mohamed Ali Pasha's country retreat a few miles north of Cairo. After more than a decade of tending to his gardens, the white-bearded Ottoman ruler of Egypt announced that he wanted a swimming pool! And not just any pool, but an enormous nymphaeum at the far end of his gardens, near a banana grove. It was to be a marble basin enclosed on four sides by frescoed galleries, with elegant kiosks in each corner, and large enough for tiny wooden rowboats and a number of marble fountains. What better place for the pasha to amuse himself with the young Circassian ladies of his harem than in the midst of cascading cool water!

Who could blame him? The foreign diplomats were calling the pasha's romantic out-of-town retreat on the Nile the "St. Cloud" of Cairo, referring to the marvelous royal park on the Seine just outside of Paris. Yet ever since the pharaohs, the Egyptians had known the name *shoubra* to mean gardens. And what gardens! The pasha's skillful gardeners from the island of Chios had worked miracles transforming thirty acres of desert into a spectacular exotic oasis at the end of a long elevated avenue from Cairo, its gigantic sycamores alone having become the talk of Europe.

On clear and balmy nights Mohamed Ali slipped out through the back door of his palace and strolled along straight allées and trellised pathways lit by gas lamps installed by his English engineer, Galloway. Paved in black and white pebble mosaics, the pathways formed tidy geometric patterns out of "a jumble of the greatest variety of plants from all parts of the old and new world," reported French horticulturist Gustave Delchevalerie. Yellow desert mimosas grew next to red ornamental hibiscus, white geraniums, and pavilions blanketed by climbing grape vines, bougainvillea and pink Laurier roses. "What roses, great God!" exclaimed the French writer Gérard de Nerval. "We can criticize the oriental taste in the interiors, but the gardens are unattackable."

Further on, enormous groves of royal Havana palms, Aleppo pines, and *Magnolia grandiflora* gave way to thick forests of olives, almonds, figs and dates, and bananas, guavas, and mangoes. "I have never seen an Oriental park with a kitchen-garden or orchard of a finer class," noted another renowned landscaper, the German Prince Hermann von Pückler-Muskau. Nicely laid-out citrus orchards bulged with a capricious planting of oranges, lemons, pomegranates, and *grenadiers*, and the finest Youssouf Effendi blood oranges, a species from Malta named after the son of an Armenian horticulturist who had brought it with him on his way back from France.

Still, no matter how pleasing his gardens and their "savage symmetry," to quote Delchevalerie, and with two elephants and a game park besides, the pasha also wanted a small Versailles. He called in Pascal Coste, a graduate of the École des Beaux-Arts in Paris, for a *pièce d'eau*, or reflecting pool, of two hundred and fifty feet by two hundred, to be supplied with water from an hydraulic steam-pump, a gift of George IV. The value of the pump—adding to the *sakiehs*, or traditional water wheels,

Statues of lions join a cavalcade of fountains whose fresh water countered the rising heat and dust in early spring when Mohamed Ali Pasha and his court moved to Shoubra Palace before going on to Ras el-Tin in Alexandria for the summer.

"Whose bubbling did a genial freshness fling," a visiting Lord Byron wrote of Mohamed Ali Pasha's marble pool and fountains, which are now being restored by the Ministry of Culture.

feeding the pasha's narrow irrigation canals and basins—was not to be lost on the engineer in Coste. For he had linked the port of Alexandria to the Nile with the seventy-five-kilometer Mamoudieh Canal, and had just begun two hundred kilometers of auxiliary waterways to make Delta cotton king in Egypt.

The young man from Marseille was not entirely happy, however. "I submitted this project at the same time as that of the palace at the Citadel, but intriguing Turkish and Armenian architects took possession of my schemes," Coste later revealed. "They only executed the grand basin, with the divan gallery . . . (and otherwise) tampered with my plans." The pasha's *Rumi* artisans indeed had substituted Coste's florid designs for the simpler yet sophisticated tastes of their Italian supervisors. Boatloads of ready-cut Carrara marble arrived from Livorno and Sicily not only for the pool but also for a magnificent circular islet and large cascading fountain, four banquettes, and a *déambulatoire*, as well as a circle of two dozen figures of crocodiles spewing out long jets of crystal-clear water.

At night under the stars and the flickering lights of Galloway Bey's gas lamps, the pasha's pool resembled the dazzling basins of Haroun el-Rachid and scenes from the *Thousand and One Nights*. Even the normally critical Gérard de Nerval softened his views on discovering the frescoed galleries draped in rich velour and lined by broad tasseled divans covered in exquisite silks. "Here, truly, was a triumph of oriental taste," he declared, entering a small salon, its ceiling of painted arabesques, geometric shapes, and theatrical masks encircled by a Greek-key border.

Elsewhere, baroque landscapes and paintings of wildlife, cheerful garlands, and portrait medallions of the pasha and his descendants enriched a décor that peaked in an impressive games room. Here neo-Pompeian nymphs floated across the ceiling above a billiards table sent by Louis-Philippe of France, its cues with sculpted bronze handles, while a *nymphaeum* in a wall niche was painted in the manner of the French master Hubert Robert. All in all, it was a setting designed to give the pasha the pleasure of watching his Circassian beauties draped in their silk peignoirs as they splashed around joyfully in four feet of water.

Was this naive
neo-Pompeian rendering
of Neptune meant to
remind Mohamed Ali Pasha
of the power of the sea
and the Mediterranean
shipping lanes that he
dreamed of controlling?

The greens, reds, and blues
add dimension to the beauty
and energy of repeating
patterns of a ceiling
decoration that in its
centerpiece pays tribute,
on the right, to Mohamed
Ali Pasha, and, to the left,
his son Ibrahim Pasha.

RAS EL-TIN PALACE

Alexandria. 1811–17; and later additions

Mohamed Ali Pasha had hired the young Italian artist on the spot. For he needed someone with just his talents, and Pietro Avoscani had not been shy about trying to get work. In the spring of 1837, at age twenty-one, he had sailed to Alexandria from Livorno to visit his brother, a distinguished commander in the Egyptian navy. With his help, indeed, he was received by the seventy-year-old Pasha of Egypt who was looking to expand and redecorate the Mediterranean palace that he had begun twenty years earlier.

The pasha's palace lay on the sandy Ras el-Tin, or Cape of Figs, of the former island of Pharos whose lighthouse was one of the ancient world's greatest wonders. The island had reconnected to the mainland in antiquity to give Alexandria its two harbors, and it was on the safer western side that Mohamed Ali had positioned his palace to overlook his new port and an arsenal for his budding navy.

At first Mohamed Ali's palace looked as if it belonged in his hometown of Cavalla on the Aegean. For his retinue of Balkan artisans had erected more of a whitewashed grange for sailors rather than a seat of power for a pasha. A simple room with plank floors served as an audience hall with a single round table and crude banquettes pushed up against bare walls. Yet rows of rectangular windows created a luminous "glass house" effect like that of the imperial palaces along the Bosphorus, prompting the pasha to take on the habits of the sultan himself. If not out in his shipyards among his workers, there he was, seated cross-legged on his great divan, peering through a telescope out to sea and pondering the fate of British admiral Lord Nelson, or the Corsican Bonaparte, who, in the pasha's own words, "had to leave Egypt like a thief in the middle of the night," for lack of a proper fleet to carry him.

The pasha had put to good use the Greeks fleeing from the wars of independence that had cost him his control of eastern Mediterranean shipping lanes. They joined in with the Italians under Avoscani's direction to transform his seaside palace into a vast seraglio. Soon rising up from afar was a long white façade, heavy gray cupolas, projecting balconies, and terraces. In Egypt, it "was the only construction of its time resembling a palace," proclaimed French engineer Linant de Bellefonds.

As de Bellefonds knew well, a "palace" in Egypt meant a Turkish *saray*—a vast residential complex, in this case, a wood-and-plaster building for the pasha's oldest son Ibrahim, another for foreign visitors and dignitaries, and a third for the ladies of the harem. Large bath houses on wooden posts, with high cupolas and crystal chandeliers, had replaced the old fishermen's huts. It was here after their baths that the ladies of the harem retreated to their *cabinets de toilette* to "drink a coffee or a syrup," reported traveler J. A. St. John, "seated on English chairs or comfy divans to be dried, fanned and perfumed by their servants." The pasha preferred to sit out on his veranda, smoking his narghile, and gauging the vessels sailing in and out of his harbor.

Mohamed Ali Pasha's palace in Alexandria stood on a "cape of figs" bound by the Mediterranean Sea on one side and, as seen here in a nineteenth-century painting, by the city's western harbor on the other. The palace was originally designed in the "Cavalla style," with a protruding upper level which typified the Macedonian houses of the pasha's hometown on the Aegean coast.

The Greeks and Italians went on to reduce the palace's excessive wall heights by filling empty surfaces with oriental fantasies and carved geometric decorations. But the big rotunda was frescoed by Avoscani himself, who later recalled that the pasha "could hardly believe his eyes." Only after the Greek consul-general at his side "ran his hand along the walls" was the pasha convinced of the joys of his trompe-l'oeil decoration!

Mountains of white plaster turned into fanciful neo-baroque moldings, and tons of Carrara marble were gobbled up for a magnificent staircase and bathrooms *à la turque*. Not everyone liked the new look, however. Prince Hermann von Pückler-Muskau, the German ambassador to the imperial Ottoman court, felt that "the eyes were offended by the bad taste of balustrades in ordinary wood and painted in white."

Still, few would have argued with the Italian traveler Baruffi who wrote in the 1840s that "the interior of the apartments offered all the luxury of the palaces of European sovereigns." The vast audience hall with its sofas in red crimson *à l'indienne* and gold cushions with foot-long fringes was "magnificent in its simplicity." And walls once graced by a single drawing of a giraffe were now covered with citations from the Koran alongside modern engravings of marine vessels and flags of naval powers.

Having lost his beloved fleet at the battle of Navarino, the pasha consoled himself with playing billiards. In the games room, a great mirror on a pivot showed on its reverse side one of his many portraits, this one the work of the painter Mayr from Munich, executed during a trip with Prince Maximilian of Bavaria in 1838.

As for Mohamed Ali's bedchamber, it was filled with "*psychés*, consoles, mirrors, and other furniture of Paris makers," according to the French artist Horace Vernet, who saw it in 1839 while on a photographic expedition. "His bed, placed in the middle, was surmounted by a vast mosquito net in gauze edged by a red ribbon border." Vernet failed to mention, however, that the pasha still slept on floor mattresses, leaving the *goût tout parisien* to his family and friends. The palace's grandest luxury was its polished parquet floors, the finest, in the audience hall, of yellow satinwood and exquisite ebony parquetry, meriting every visitor's footstep to be dutifully wiped away by a close following of domestics.

The greater the pasha's military successes, the greater his gifts from afar. A table of precious stones arrived from Pope Gregory XVI, in gratitude for the four magnificent alabaster columns the pasha had sent to Rome for the reconstruction of the basilica of Saint Paul. The East India Company delivered a ten-foot-high fountain in solid silver. Pendulum clocks came from England and Russia, and a magnificent Sèvres porcelain table service from King Louis-Philippe of France. There were gilt-bronze Empire chandeliers, a rare chimney-piece of black marble, and mahogany and glass cabinets for trophy birds, mounted by the best artisans of Europe. A smoking room housed unique specimens of Turkish pipes—jasmine wood *chubouks* covered with gold filigree and decked out with gems.

All of this gave the pasha tremendous pride when the Ottoman fleet pulled into port in 1839, and its officers stampeded the entrance doors to his palace. By then Avoscani was gone, but Mohamed Ali, the man of war, had become a man of culture. His face broke out into a thin smile as he caressed his white beard and remarked to an aide: "They have reason to want to enter. They want to see something that is not seen every day."

HOSH AL-BASHA

Southern Cemetery, Cairo. Circa 1820 and thereafter

It was silent, solemn, and imposing. And it was vast—with a number of irregular rooms and five cupolas in the Constantinoplitan style.

The stone structure was the work of Greeks and Armenians. Inside were rich Persian carpets, windows covered in green silk, large cashmere shawls, cushions and divans for the niches, even small chairs. Splendid chandeliers hung from high vaulted ceilings to flood the rooms with delicately filtered light. Outside was a charming courtyard with trees and parterres of flowers. The entire complex was perfectly positioned just behind the mausoleum of Imam al-Shaf'i, one of the four founders of Sunni Islam, who had died in 820. It was little surprise that the building intended as Mohamed Ali Pasha's final resting place was also for some years his favorite place to visit while he was alive.

As the Ottoman sultan's viceroy of Egypt, Mohamed Ali naturally had wanted to build his family tomb on the grandest imaginable scale. He planned his mausoleum right next to the largest Islamic mortuary chamber in Egypt, celebrated for its magnificent lead-sheathed wooden dome painted in red, blue, and gold in a rising floral pattern. Was it not here that the great ruler Saladin had founded the first *madrasa* to counter the teachings of the Fatimid Shi'ites? The significance of this was not lost on Mohamed Ali who had sent his son Toussoun on a victorious campaign against the radical Wahabis in the Hejaz, only to see him die of the plague in 1816 at age twenty-three. Toussoun was the first in the family to be interred in the tomb.

By the time the English traveler Sarah Lushington arrived in 1827, the pasha's mausoleum "constituted one of the curiosities of Cairo." There were "splendid tombs of marble," decorated in yellow, blue, and red, and washed in gold. They held not only Toussoun, but also the remains of his younger brother Ismail, who had been burnt alive in the Sudan in 1822 at age twenty-seven. Steps away lay the body of the pasha's beloved sister, and, occupying the place of honor, was Amina, the pasha's first and favorite wife, who had died in 1824. Mohamed Ali had so many reasons to devote what time he could to communing with these dear shades, and with the promise of his own future glory.

For many visitors, the success of the plan was complete. Mrs. Lushington was captivated: "The tombs, in marble, resembling altars, are flanked at the head and feet by a stele or column according to the Turkish mode; the column at the head ends in a coiffure distinctive of the rank or gender of the deceased." A sculpted turban or fez denoted a man, a vase or a coronet, a lady. Quotations from the Koran were inscribed in the stone, along with flowers, often with emblematic meanings; the tombs of young girls were adorned with roses.

A few years later J. A. St. John deemed the "mortuary columns, as well as the sarcophagi covered in Turkish or Arab inscriptions in golden lettering, intermingled with flowers and different capricious designs, to be of the most pleasing effect."

Ottoman "umbrella" domes and stone masonry in the Mameluke style made the family tomb of Mohamed Ali Pasha, in its day, the greatest monument of modern Egypt. The pasha's personal retinue of Mamelukes, or "slave warriors," who were of French origin, had their cenotaphs in an adjoining garden.

Around the tomb of Amina now were many others in the family, with final resting places that were "elegant, in good taste, full of melancholy, in the middle of all this gilded ornament." For St. John, the entire ensemble certainly seemed "majestic."

For the French poet and traveler Gérard de Nerval, the monument struck quite a different, and unsettling, note. By the time of his visit, the mausoleum contained more than sixty tombs of all different shapes and sizes. Seeing all the columns with their turbans and coronets, even tresses, created an effect that was almost surreal: "It seemed as if we were walking through a petrified crowd."

Perhaps something of that uncanny, even tragic, atmosphere registered with the mausoleum's creator. For in the end, after all the years he had spent erecting this monument to his family's glory, Mohamed Ali built a great alabaster mosque inside the walls of the Citadel, and it was here, in a magnificent white tomb, that he himself was buried in 1848.

The entry corridor to Mohamed Ali Pasha's family mausoleum testifies to an orderly and rational transit from the present world into the one of spiritual splendor inside.

All of the color, fluidity, and form of the Ottoman Turkish baroque is here for the tomb of Mohamed Ali Pasha's favorite wife, Amina. Running down the back side of its column, in stucco, is a single long braid of hair.

Greek and Armenian stone-
masons from Istanbul
chiseled out geometric
patterns, vertical contour
molding, and suspended
stalactite formations that
recall the Middle Mameluke
style, and which together
exude a powerful presence.

Tarbooshes and turbans
for the men, vases and
coronets for the ladies, amid
a profusion of acanthus
garlands, fronds, leaves and
stems, and poetic verses,
gave French visitor Gérard
de Nerval the idea that
this tomb had the
"atmosphere of a city."

MONASTERLY SALAMLIK

Roda Island, Cairo. Early 1860s

H asan Pasha's couriers suddenly rushed in to show him the latest *Journal de Constantinople*. It seemed that a French journalist had undergone a dramatic change of heart after visiting the island of Roda. What could have gone wrong? Gérard de Nerval had been charmed by the island in the Nile across from ancient Babylon. Here, he told his readers, you could find not only Ibrahim Pasha's "delicious princely residence," but also "the Jardin des Plantes of Cairo." Replacing the pleasure gardens of the Mameluke sultans were a thousand species of exotic trees and plants from around the world—crammed into two immense gardens, one French, the other English.

Hasan Pasha smiled to himself. For he was sure that de Nerval had visited the northern end of the island to see its English garden—laid out like the jungles of Bengal, with unimaginable foliage and bizarre fruits. The only thing missing was the tigers. "Ibrahim was happiest cultivating the plants of India," de Nerval observed, before launching into a more lyrical note: "Between the stones, at the sides of the paths, over our heads, under our feet, writhing, embracing, bristling, grimacing, were the strangest reptiles of the vegetal world."

But why then finish on a note of cold mockery? For the newspaper had reprinted de Nerval's letter to a French friend: "Don't bother coming to see the island of Roda which has been transformed into an English garden by Ibrahim, with artificial streams, the odd lawn and the occasional Chinese bridge."

As Hasan had feared, the truth had been revealed. In the early 1830s, the ruler he served, Mohamed Ali Pasha, had hired an English gardener who took his inspiration from nature more than art. No reason prevailed over the planting of huge clusters of trees of wildly varying sizes. Venerable sycamores were stolen of their rightful beauty by a curtain of poplars and weeping willows; pine trees shot up so high as to entirely block the pathways! And the tiny streams—projecting the luxury of tropical vegetation and flowing capriciously through man-made rolling green lawns—led not to rustic perspectives, but—in Egypt, of all places!—only to fake ruins of temples and other monuments!

It was no surprise to Hasan Pasha that the visiting Prince Hermann von Pückler-Muskau would be even more direct in his criticism. "This delicious island, richly wooded, was unfortunately spoiled some time ago by the absurd idea of making what they call a garden or an English park," declared the friend of Mohamed Ali. "The result is deplorable. . . . For the trees are not distributed like ours across a meadow or clearing, but strewn around potato fields and cabbage patches."

Hasan Pasha was not about to make the same mistake. Here, on the far southern side of Roda, where the river spreads its arms wide, and the scorching wind of the desert always turns fresh, here where one could not help but feel so much at home and alive, Hasan was building himself a magnificent Turkish *saray* in the grand style of the late Ottoman baroque.

The result was like nothing else to be seen in Egypt. With his property of seven *feddans* bound by the river on three

The Ottoman pasha Hasan, a native of Monastir in the hills of Macedonia above northern Greece—a region once called Eastern Rumelia and possessed by the Turks before later being incorporated into Bulgaria—built his *salamlik* only yards away from the Nilometer. This measuring device for five thousand years had indicated the level of the annual floods of the river that would make or break the Egyptian agricultural economy.

To the fanciful arabesques of a ceiling decoration was added a touch of the grotesque: the mythological griffin, a symbol of protection, and, in Egypt, one that specifically denotes dominance over the sky and earth.

The European windows of the great reception hall illuminate a rococo turquoise-green palette that appears more lively than the somber green of the *salamlik's* side rooms.

From the southern tip of Roda Island, the *salamlik* built by Hasan Pasha overlooks the widest part of the Nile in Cairo and is the site where, according to well-known legends, the pharaoh's daughter found the infant Moses in a basket on a shore fringed by reeds.

sides, Hasan Pasha needed only to erect a high stone wall to cut him off from the rest of the island. A huge *haramlik* for his family had a double staircase in marble, and lofty wooden verandas with curved overhangs so typical of the Ottoman period. Inside, as if rectangular windows and jalousies in the European style could not give enough views of the greenery and water, huge gilded mirrors on the walls amplified the light.

Hasan also built a round white kiosk encircled by a columned veranda for taking the sun in winter. When summer came, there was a second kiosk, painted red, positioned to receive the full benefit of the cooling northern breezes coming off the water.

But it was in 1851 at the water's edge to the south that the real pride of the *saray* appeared in a *salamlik* for public functions. The reception house opened its doors to reveal enormous rooms in lively rococo colors—blue and pinks and greens—and huge gilded divans. Here Hasan would hold his official meetings, first as prime minister to Mohamed Ali's successor, Abbas Hilmi I, and later as governor of Cairo. As custodian of the Nilometer that was located only yards away, he also presided over the ceremonies observed at the time of the annual floods, which Egypt's farmers had counted on since antiquity.

And the gardens? "Fruits!" proclaimed Hasan's great-great-granddaughter Fatma, the last person to live in the complex before Nasser's revolution. Nothing more? "Only fruits—dates, mangoes, guavas, strawberries, blackberries, and blueberries," she insisted. For Hasan had lived long enough to see the Nile floods wreck Ibrahim Pasha's celebrated garden. Except for the tallest specimens, most of the plants had been swept away shortly after his death.

MENA HOUSE

Pyramids, Giza. 1867–69

H ad it really been forty years? It seemed like only yesterday that the Empress Eugénie had sailed up the Nile for what was to be the time of her life. How could she forget the stop at Luxor? It had been late October and more than ninety-six degrees in her cabins when the telegram arrived from her husband telling her that in Paris it was snowing!

The Khedive Ismail had thought of everything. Awaiting her out in the desert at Saqqara were billowing silk tents, some lined in sumptuous yellow satin, others in red, all with matching sofas and cushions. Reaching the Giza plateau at nightfall, after trekking across twenty miles of desert by donkey, she saw the Sphinx and Khufu's Great Pyramid brought to life under a burst of magnesium flares. And then, with *machallahs* or torches, lighting the way, Ismail himself had led her down from the plateau to his charming chalet to take a rest before she returned to Cairo.

Revisiting the scene in 1909, Eugénie surely recalled her sumptuous pyramids dinner, and a creamy Turkish dessert known as *Om Ali*. Now more than eighty, her hair gone gray, and her eyesight failing, she could not be faulted for failing to recognize Ismail's rest house that had hosted her and other royal guests attending the khedive's gala Suez Canal opening. Times had changed, and so had the owners—more than once. In a word, the British had arrived. And their style and tastes were here to stay.

Yes, the wide desert and its great monuments were still there, as were Bedouins for neighbors. But curtains and cushions were now in pretty patterned chintzes, and a library offered a selection of English books. Quaint wooden verandas extending off the bed chambers made a relaxing setting for "English breakfast" and the morning's *Egyptian Gazette*. And a terrace filled with small tables and big wicker armchairs allowed a hundred people to take afternoon tea together to the sound of orchestral strings, and under the shadows of one of the ancient world's greatest wonders. Not all, however, was destined to be so Victorian. For the rest house that Ismail originally had built as a hunting lodge for himself and his friends to see the pyramids, or shoot quail flying north in the spring and ducks in the autumn flood season, had been reincarnated as a great hotel. And on the very spot where the lodge once stood was a spectacular dining room with a high domed ceiling to look like the inside of a mosque!

Could the Khedive Ismail ever have imagined that his simple hunting lodge at the foot of the Great Pyramids would go on to host the world's kings and queens, political leaders, army generals, movie stars, and socialites?

Ethel Locke-King and her husband Hugh had revolutionized the spacious mansion owned originally by another wealthy young couple, Frederick Head and his Australian wife. The Heads had come to Egypt, as would the Locke-Kings after them, for the health benefits of its sunny dry climate. The Heads had added a first floor to gain an uninterrupted view of the pyramids across the date palms and gardens planted with oleanders, hibiscus, and roses. Keeping many of Ismail's precious Eastern treasures and buying a few of their own, they did not hesitate when the eminent Orientalist Archibald Henry Sayce suggested naming their new residence Mena House after the first of the seventy-six kings of ancient Egypt.

"Everything is original," declares Samir Zakhary, an expert on oriental furniture, who further notes that Mena House's oversized cabinets, canapés, and side chairs are in the Coptic style and "inlaid with mother-of-pearl, and not ivory, but camel bone." The upper gallery likely originated from an old palace in Rosetta or Damietta.

Horseshoe arches, *mashrabiya* screens, and chairs in the Mameluke style —and said to be Egypt's first seating along Western lines since the pharaohs— were most probably crafted by Jewish artisans, and went far to convince visitors that this was the East.

This pierced-metal lantern typifies the Mameluke taste for large and bold Arabic inscriptions.

It was more than a good decade before the turn of the century when the Locke-Kings had taken full charge of the place, and Ethel commissioned architect Henri Favarger to design the hotel's dining room. For this, the London resident had rerouted the most fashionable trend in the West back to the East by creating a great hall within a hall, and accenting keyhole arches and plain plaster walls with one of the glories of medieval oriental craftsmanship—the screens and windows of turned wood known as *mashrabiya*. A galaxy of antique Islamic lanterns suspended from the ceiling also added to Favarger's fancy, and doubtless contributed to the success of his application for a fellowship at the Royal Institute of British Architects.

For the Locke-Kings, the pyramids house solved their problem of finding suitable accommodation for the six-months-plus winter "season." As the daughter of a governor of both New South Wales and New Zealand, Ethel had traveled extensively. The idea of turning the first residential house beside the pyramids into a luxurious hotel thus came naturally to her. "Money was no object, and they spared none in carrying out their idea," reported society observer Mabel Caillard.

The Locke-Kings planned to create one of the world's most exclusive hotels—and one of the first to have a swimming pool. They "envisaged a combination of English comfort with Arab decoration," declared Mrs. Caillard. With large rectangular windows and French doors, and no Western-style shutters to speak of, they added velvet curtains and built great log fires for the cold desert nights. Still, they worked hard to keep the original oriental character with its echoes of medieval Islamic Cairo, hoping to make it, as Mrs. Caillard added, "a veritable museum of Arab art." They bought narrow wooden balconies with *mashrabiyas*—originally used for cooling jugs of water—which they often found intact in the homes of medieval merchants in the northern Delta. They also refitted ancient wooden chairs and couches for their Old Bar, and covered walls with old Turkish-blue tiles as well as mosaics of colored stones.

The complex soon also included a villa, stables, a police post, and garden kiosks. This was the grand hotel greeting Eugénie on her second visit. One thing she still could see well enough was that Mena House stood a cut above the other hotels in Cairo, where over-plastered pharaonic motifs were already considered the height of fashion.

GEZIRA PALACE

Zamalek, Cairo. 1863–69

The Khedive Ismail's hopes rose to the sky, his heart pounded faster at each passing moment. Nor could the heavy mist along the Mediterranean coast dampen his spirits. For the imperial yacht *L'Aigle* carrying the beautiful Empress Eugénie had set anchor in the port of Alexandria just before dawn that third Friday in October 1869. The short and stocky khedive, at age thirty-nine, could hardly wait to receive the empress of France who had captivated him two years earlier at the Exposition Universelle in Paris. Now she was to be his guest of honor among the rulers of Europe attending the gala opening of the Suez canal built by her cousin, Ferdinand de Lesseps.

Traveling privately in a simple gray dress and small straw hat, looking like any first-time visitor to the land of the pharaohs, Eugénie stepped ashore to take Ismail's arm onto an awaiting train for Cairo. Hardly could she imagine what was in store for her even in advance of the formal festivities.

Ismail had gone to great length to impress the former Spanish countess of Montijo who had pushed hard for her cousin and his canal, even changing her husband's mind about the former diplomat, once persona non grata in Second Empire circles. Now de Lesseps had the full support of the French government, his canal was owned and operated by French interests, and in selling off his shares, Ismail had become, at least temporarily, a French satellite.

As they arrived in the capital, Ismail skirted around the giant construction site that was his New Cairo in the works on former marsh lands. In the midst of building a city modeled on modern Paris, with grand boulevards, a *bourse*, theaters, and an opera house, Ismail also had erected palaces, some thirty across Egypt, and six in Cairo alone. "Every man," he would say in French, speaking with a slight Italian accent, "is mad about some one subject. My mania is for stone." However, as he later would confide, "I had not more than eight palaces ready for the sovereigns and princes honoring me by coming for the occasion of the opening of the canal."

The palace of Abdin was still not complete, and Verdi would not have Aïda ready in time for the new opera house. But the rush was on to transform Ismail's palace on an island in the Nile for Eugénie's stay of three days in Cairo. Much needed to be done on this once desolate *gezira*—an island of muddy fields and lanky date-palms, where, in 1830, Ismail's grandfather Mohamed Ali Pasha had asked the decorator Pietro Avoscani to design him a simple *haramlik* for the ladies of his harem and a billet for his guards. These buildings would give the island's northern end the Turkish name *Zamalek*, "habitation of fortune."

Ismail guided the empress into an open carriage, escorting her to the port of Boulaq and across the water by barge to his newly refitted palace. Here was not just one building, but a vast compound of reception houses, private quarters, annexes, garden kiosks, and assorted auxiliary buildings—a Turkish *saray* worthy of the *Thousand and One Nights*, but with every

More than three dozen courses were served to five thousand guests at the opening of the Suez Canal, among them, as depicted in this modern rendering, the Khedive Ismail, on the right, wearing a red tarboosh, and, at center, with her back turned, the French empress, Eugénie, with her cousin, the canal-builder Ferdinand de Lesseps, seated at her left.

43

The marble eagle and lions of the great marble staircase assured the Khedive Ismail's guests from Europe that this Gezira Island palace had been built for a true sovereign.

Did the Khedive Ismail favor the color green because of its symbolism of divine providence? And gold because of its attachment to royal rule? Or were his Italian architects, engineers, and decorators simply trying to upstage the Germans who were muscling in on their schemes and plans for his Gezira Island palace?

The porticoes for the Gezira Palace of the Khedive Ismail were created by architect Carl von Diebitsch several years after he had designed a cast-iron staircase and a huge pillared hall for his minister Sherif Pasha—a work that brought him praise from Berlin's discerning art magazine *Dioskuren*. A pair of cast-iron *mashrabiya* doorways, also for Sherif and the mausoleum of his father-in-law, Soliman Pasha el-Faransawy, became the prototype for his "modern" Moorish kiosk at the Paris Exposition of 1867.

modern convenience. This had become Ismail's favorite summer retreat after a fortune teller had predicted he would meet his fate in the Mediterranean port of Alexandria.

A big, bold palace hugged the shoreline in front of Eugénie like the grand foyer of a spectacular outdoor theater, rolling out a carpet of forty-some acres of parks and gardens. Night fell only to be taken back by garlands of multi-colored lights, Venetian lanterns, and magnesium torches—going far to impress an empress who thought she had seen everything in the glittering lights of Paris. There was an aquarium, and a zoo of African reptiles and beasts—tigers, bears, giraffes, ostriches, and gazelles, not to mention rare birds, including hundreds of pink flamingoes—all enclosed by gilded grillwork recalling the elegant Parc Monceau of Paris.

Ismail had not skimped on any detail to make both the empress and the Spaniard in Eugénie feel at home. At her disposal was an entire wing of his palace, known as the *salamlik*, where she and other guests were kept at a distance from Ismail's household of wives, concubines, children, and servants. They were confined to the shuttered—and well guarded—*haramlik*, or family quarters, hidden behind banyan trees and high stone walls.

Redecorating the *salamlik* for Eugénie had been neither fast nor easy. Ismail had asked his architect Julius Franz, who had trained at the polytechnic and art academy of Vienna, to supervise. The palace's glamour, however, would come from German architect Carl von Diebitsch who had what Ismail wanted most to impress Eugénie: an exciting way of reviving the best of Moorish Spain.

Von Diebitsch was to make his mark absolute and immediate. At the entrance door to Eugénie's wing stood a spectacular cast-iron portico that had for its ancestor the famous patio of the Lions at the Alhambra. On the garden side were three more Moorish porticoes to serenade the empress with a cantata of light set to elegant horseshoe arches and columns, punctuated in a delicate relief of arabesques and stalactites. Prefabricated by von Diebitsch in iron at the Lauchhammer factories near Dresden, the porticoes had been packed into numbered kits and shipped to Cairo for reassembly. Perfect for the balconies that Franz needed for his first-floor doors and windows, they also proved just right for a monumental garden kiosk farther inside the gardens, near a small lake. Here the *Nimsawi* ("the Austrian") Franz, as Arabic speakers called him, had built a long, narrow summer palace that for him was "probably the finest modern Arabian structure of its kind." Its marvelous open vestibule featured views of lush green verdure, its gently rippling water from a marble fountain casting a magic spell beneath von Diebitsch's tall, cast-iron arches that also recalled the Alhambra—the result of six months the architect had spent at the Moorish palace on a red hill-top overlooking the Granada plain.

Shortly after arriving, Eugénie wrote to her husband Louis-Napoleon: "Cairo has conserved its ancient cachet . . . which for me recalls Spain. The dances, the music, and the food are identical . . . Today I'm staying put for a rest, because I'm very tired, but very interested by all that I see."

Others were interested, but not impressed. Society observer Mabel Caillard later dismissed the buildings as "cardboard monuments," complaining that the European contractors, "so long as they could satisfy the eye of their munificent employer by external ornamentation, cared little for the rules of art or the principles of solid construction." Indeed, the gorgeous lath-and-plaster residences barely outlasted their predecessors. By 1878, Ismail was bankrupt, and his summer retreat had reverted to the state. And von Diebitsch died unexpectedly at age fifty from an attack of smallpox before the canal festivities even began.

ABDIN PALACE

Cairo. 1863–74

Silence reigned over the crowned heads of Europe as the Swiss chamberlain cried out, "Sa Majesté, le Roi d'Égypte!" Even Ismail Pasha, himself, the Ottoman viceroy of Egypt, was startled by the unexpected salutation. For he knew that his nominal sovereign, Sultan Abdul-Aziz, was soon to arrive in Paris for the Exposition Universelle. He also knew that appearances counted for everything, and secretly he was elated by the latest developments. The imperial *firman* granting him a new title, negotiated by his minister Nubar Pasha only days earlier in Istanbul, was already taking hold.

Ismail Pasha, then thirty-seven, had become the first khedive of Egypt. And to his delight, the Persian title of *kiva*, or "divine one," bestowed on him by his first cousin Abdul-Aziz, also had come with the manner of address that he coveted most: that of El-Aziz, or His Highness. "Purely honorific, Sire," the wily Armenian Nubar would reply to an inquisitive Louis Napoleon. "The importance of the *firman*," he went on, "is that it constitutes the complete autonomy of Egypt, and accords the right to the khedive to make trade conventions."

It was a major victory for the Khedive Ismail, who returned to Egypt with the idea that if he was not a king, at least he could look like one, and one living in a modern-day capital. No matter the cost, or the state of his finances, he was determined to have a new Cairo in the image of Louis Napoleon's Paris of broad new boulevards, squares, and parks. First on the list was to move his seat of power from the out-of-the-way Citadel complex built by his grandfather Mohamed Ali Pasha.

Ismail wanted a new palace for his new city, with an opera house, theater, and hippodrome. But more than a decade was to pass before the house and grounds of Abdin Bey, an Albanian commander of the Ottoman sultan's guard, were plowed under along with surrounding streets to make way for a sprawling khedival complex fronted by a grand esplanade. The future five-hundred-room monstrosity was far from the first neoclassical building, which was not even finished in time for the gala Suez Canal opening. Yet remaining in memory of the event's guest of honor, the Empress Eugénie, was a majestic ceremonial gate, Bab Paris.

Much as the khedive loved public grandeur, his working space and private apartments were modest. His audience chamber held little pretension: a Persian carpet, a damask-covered divan, a few chairs and curtains in a matching fabric, half a dozen crystal sconces on arabesque walls, and a small gilt table. A small dining area overlooked a winter garden—a gallery flanked at either end by marble busts of Marie Antoinette and the Empress Eugénie.

So delighted was the Khedive Ismail with his Abdin Palace that he wanted to keep the complex as his own personal property rather than have it go to the state—to which it belongs to this day.

Besides his French engineers led by Léon Rousseau Pasha, the ruler Ismail maintained a host of Italian builders and decorators who produced a long suite of rooms, one more dazzling than another. Among them was a Giuseppe Garozzo, a Sicilian from Catania, and founder of Cairo's largest construction company; and Ciro Pantanelli, whose keen eye for Islamic styles had been formed by his studies at the Royal Institute of Arts in Siena. The busy atelier of Giuseppe Parvis on the edge

The Bab Paris or Paris Gate, built in honor of the Empress Eugénie's visit in 1869, today is used as the entrance to the public portions of the palace and its grounds.

of Islamic Cairo could not have been further removed in atmosphere from his study halls at the Albertine Academy in Turin or the Beaux-Arts in Paris, yet the setting was to be inspirational. For Parvis and his sons were to turn out original, world-class furniture, Giuseppe himself producing an exquisite oriental suite that would be awarded a gold medal at the 1867 Paris Exposition.

Elio Prinzavalli's painted inscriptions, intricate marquetry, and fine wood carving provided Ismail the finest hall of his palace, the spectacular Throne Room. The lofty reception halls often stood silent, except for occasional noon luncheons; formal dinners *à la française* were served at seven p.m. on vast numbers of Turkish plates and crystal glassware, each marked with a golden "I" surmounted by a crown. There was French champagne and Ismail's favorite Château d'Yquem for special occasions and an "in season" crowd that included Egyptians who dressed and ate in the European manner. Before a great neo-baroque theater was added, musical evenings and balls began in a main hall at nine and ended after midnight. And Ismail always invited the ladies, court etiquette having shifted to the *style à l'anglaise*.

After a fire struck in 1891, Ismail's son and successor tried to enlist the talents of Carl von Hasenauer, the leading architect of Vienna's Ringstrasse. Busy with his work on Vienna's Museum of Fine Arts, he instead sent his star pupil, a nineteen-year-old Joseph Urban, who added a new four-story western wing to the palace within eight months. Twenty years later, Ismail's grandson, Abbas Hilmi II, ordered a total reconstruction by his architect Antonio Lasciac. Later, when Ismail's youngest son, Fuad, came to rule after growing up in Italy, he ordered further renovations from his court architect, Ernesto Verrucci Bey. He created a luxurious neo-Byzantine hall inlaid with mosaics, alabaster, and marble—a fitting addition to what by then had become the palace of the first King of Egypt.

ANTONIADIS VILLA AND GARDENS

Nouzha, Alexandria. Circa 1865

At age fourteen, in 1833, with an Ottoman *laissez-passer* tucked inside his shirt pocket, the future Sir John Antoniadis sailed away from his home on the Aegean island of Lemnos with few intentions of returning. An uncle in Alexandria had sent for him. Now, thirty-two years later, with the azure Mediterranean sea and sky before him, he recalled the day of his arrival. The port of Alexandria was abuzz with seafaring vessels, and the docks rang out with the lingua franca of seamen. Nearly everyone on the streets spoke Italian, which Sir John also would pick up fast and put to use later in his trading with Livorno. Italian also was good for ordering lunch at Cirioni's, and meeting shipping agents after dinner at the Café de France.

Luckily, Sir John had taken the flag of his half-Russian mother, and he went on to trade grains with Odessa, as well as deal with South Africa, and the East India Company. Yet, he always thought of himself as a Greek, and as Greek as any other of the Orthodox families who had adopted Alexandria as their own. His people were the Tossizzas from Epirus, Jean d'Anastasy of Salonika, the Zizinia brothers transplanted to Marseille after being chased by the Turks from their native Chios to become Belgian consuls and titled counts. Sir John saw how they all had done well by serving Mohamed Ali Pasha, trading his grains and other commodities to British Malta, in return for the most precious ingredient of any new-born power: arms and ammunition.

The cotton boom arrived to make all the Greeks with big names great barons. Among them was Sir John, who also started developing urban properties, and helped found the Bank of Alexandria. When the inevitable bust brought revolt, prompting the British to arrive offshore with raised guns, he came forth ready and able with offers of assistance. In 1887 General Wolseley invested him into knighthood by the order of Queen Victoria.

In the days before Alexandria had paved roads and gaslights, Sir John had acquired a rambling property of twenty-five acres on the Mamoudieh Canal, originally the personal domain of Mohamed Ali Pasha. Here, with sycamores and pepper trees sweeping down over its high muddy banks, the canal known as the Champs-Élysées of Alexandria offered romantic promenades and picnics on Friday or Sunday afternoons, and good terrain for pigeon-shooting at anytime.

Mohamed Ali had granted lands along the canal to his family, and friends who often doubled as his commercial agents. Among them was François Bravay, an adventurer from Marseille, court jester, and "fixer" of the first order. Bravay had befriended Mohamed Ali's son, Said Pasha, who had come to rule as viceroy of Egypt to discover that his financial ills could not be cured by a perfect command of French and exquisite manners. Said Pasha's treasury was depleted, and bankers on three continents were pressing him badly. He had no choice but to liquidate the estate of a family member who had squandered a spectacular fortune. Up for sale was a huge building in the city's European quarter, as well as the old terrains of Mohamed Ali. To the rescue came Bravay with a fabulously liquid Sir John, waiting happily in the wings to pick up properties at a price far below their real market value.

A landscaping plan of 1890 signed by the Greek architect Pericles Lascaris does not rule out contributions to the Antoniadis grounds from others, such as Belgian landscaper Monfront Bey, and later, another Belgian, the director of Alexandria's parks and gardens, Paul Richard. Taken over subsequently by the governor of Alexandria, the grounds were opened to the public; here in 1936, Britain signed a treaty to withdraw its military forces from Egypt; and an ordinance was drafted that gave birth to the modern Olympic games.

ABOVE
Did an Italian architect design this villa on the banks of the Mamoudieh Canal? The answer remains a mystery. But statues of the Four Seasons in niches near the roof remain as a symbol of the Italian Renaissance and its idea of cosmic order and the repeating cycles of spring, summer, autumn, and winter that represent human life and the expectation of spiritual if not actual rebirth—thoughts not lost on a native of the Aegean island of Lemnos who was Sir John Antoniadis.

Lord Nelson was one of six marble statues commissioned by the painter and decorator Pietro Avoscani in the late 1850s and executed by Italian sculptors for the suburban Alexandria palace of the viceroy Said Pasha, the son of the great Mohamed Ali Pasha.

OPPOSITE
Sir John Antoniadis's sponsorship of a five-volume illustrated *History of Greece* in 1865 coincided with his purchase of a country estate in what was once the ancient Ptolemaic suburb of Eleusis and home to the third-century-BC poet Callimachos—and a perfect setting for seventeen marble statues, among them the Venus of Roman myth (Aphrodite *in naturalis)*, to the benefit of guests such as the Shah of Iran and Princess Fawzia of Egypt, the sister of King Farouk, who stayed here on their honeymoon.

Sir John thus came into a new town house in the city as well as a suburban property where he drew from the Renaissance to build himself a version of Cliveden. Soon terraced lawns with elegant balustrades had gone in, amid towering royal palms, and heroic statuary displayed the modern glory of Alexandria. A new neighbor also was to be had in Said Pasha's successor, the Khedive Ismail. Sir John became a favorite of the new ruler's household, and he went on to host a grand banquet and ball for Ismail that became the talk of Alexandria for at least the next half century.

In 1890, with Alexandria booming once again after the British bombardment, a Greek designer and others were asked to further embellish Sir John's country estate. Eclecticism reached new heights in tall Andalusian walls defending romantic waterfalls and fountains; greenery formed decorative circles, squares, and pyramids; marble sculptures graced terraces recalling Caserta, while water views offered the finest of French perspectives, and English-style natural planting followed curved pathways to recall St. James Park. All of this complemented the circular arrangement fronting the villa, where six marble statues had been transferred from Said Pasha's former palace: renditions of Christopher Columbus, Vasco de Gama, Admiral Lord Nelson, and the French naval commander Jean Bart, as well as allegories of astronomy and seafaring.

Statues of the Four Seasons stood like sentries in niches along the upper walls of the two-storied villa. In the distance, to one side, a glass planetarium flickered under the lights near an open-air bandstand with a theater and backdrop of Greek columns resembling the ancient Roman stage at Baalbek. In another direction rolled out flower beds of scarlet gladioli and red roses, yellow mimosas, and red euphoria; and, further on, groves of royal palm trees, bananas, cactus, bamboo, and aloe. Heralded by a symphony of seven fountains, Aphrodite, the goddess of love and joy, long gone from the island of Lemnos, was reborn to meet up with Artemis and Eros in the main gardens of Sir John Antoniadis. For she reminded him of home.

THE KHEDIVE ISMAIL'S REST HOUSE

Armant, province of Qena. 1860s

The Khedive Ismail suddenly pushed aside the papers in front of him. The situation was alarming. Exports of Egyptian sugar had dried up almost entirely, and French imports were flooding the local market. This was an unexpected crisis. After all, sugar was not new to Egypt. Had not his father, Ibrahim Pasha, reintroduced the refining of raw sugar into crystals after a lapse of centuries? What now was Ismail to do? "Our harvest of cane is magnificent and the return on sugar is mediocre. Why?" he lamented.

Ismail decided to beat the French at their own game in "white gold" by starting a modern sugar industry. He combined his vast estates in middle and upper Egypt into one giant plantation, and ordered the building of sixteen factories in the fertile corridor along the upper Nile. Many millions of francs were spent on new machines from France, although some did not function properly and had to be put out for scrap soon after their installation.

A frantic rush was on in a country where no rain fell for most of the year. The need for water to grow the cane in summer led to the Ibrahimiya Canal, just as the sweet water Ismailiya was being cut in the eastern Delta. Steam pumps were ordered, and railway lines laid. Not surprisingly, more capital was needed, and Ismail borrowed against his estates so that soon a loan of 175 million francs was emitted from Paris.

With so much at stake, Ismail gave nothing less than his personal attention to every detail of his massive agricultural undertaking. It was only natural then that he also should desire the comfort of a rest house for his inspection trips down south. Besides, the area around Armant was good for shooting ducks in winter while the cane harvest was in progress. And what could be better than a picturesque spot on the west bank of the Nile, where crested hoopoes flew over the sturdy tall brakes of sugar cane. Here too, in the outskirts of ancient Hermonthis, his grandfather Mohamed Ali Pasha had built one of his first two sugar plants using stones from Cleopatra's temple!

Ismail built a factory for "white" raw sugar, as well as an annex to distill "red" cane into molasses and alcohol. In doing so, he had followed the lead of his father Ibrahim's planting of a variety of "red" cane from Jamaica and added two new strains, the "Bourbon" and "Otahiti," for cultivation in and around Armant.

By the time Ismail had finished at Armant, the French engineers who had turned the canal cities of Port Said and Ismailiya into a place very much like the French Quarter of New Orleans had left their stamp on the new project. For among the lanky date palms and lush foliage rose up a rest house with a wide pitched roof, and a big front veranda standing on high wooden stilts! A second veranda one level higher offered views of the river lined with avenues of sycamore figs, the desert beyond, and distant mountains.

Thick-walled rooms opening one into another dispelled the heat build-up in the southern summers, and fireplaces kept

Nile flotillas passed just in front of the Khedive Ismail's rest house that later turned into the residence of another "sugar king," the twentieth-century entrepreneur Abboud Pasha.

The Khedive Ismail's rest house at Armant resembled the colonial residences of the French workers employed by Ferdinand de Lesseps to build his canal through the Suez isthmus between the Mediterranean and the Red Sea.

OPPOSITE
The rooms of the Khedive Ismail's rest house rose five meters high and flowed one into another to allow maximum light and volume for air circulation that was so vital in the hot, dry climate of upper Egypt.

the night chill away. A narrow staircase winding up a tower made it clear that this was a place for the few rather than many to enjoy sweet-smelling jasmine and jacarandas amid the bougainvillea and tamarisks by the river.

A sense of pride came over Ismail as European guests visiting the country for the opening of his Suez Canal sailed past his rest house. Among those touring upper Egypt were members of the French Institute, men of letters, his guest of honor the Empress Eugénie, the Jockey Club crowd, and a gaggle of German consultants. They would visit the *sucrerie* at Roda, but it was at Armant, the "southern Heliopolis," that they would see a sun temple dedicated to Egypt's sugar king, the Khedive Ismail.

ABD EL-RAZIK SALAMLIK

Abu Gerg, province of Minya. Circa 1860

The table was laid at four or five in the afternoon when everyone came in from the fields. Grandmother Safia always cooked half a lamb, and each house would send over a tray. All the necessities were easily available. "We could live without going out," Adel Mohamed Abd el-Razik proclaimed. "We grew fruits and vegetables. In the yard we had horses and camels. We had our own bakery, our own sugar cane press. And we were famous for the sugar cane. It was unlike anything else in the world."

Indeed, the Abd el-Raziks' sugar was unique, as was their cotton, and their land. "It was a sacred area," their descendant went on reflectively. El-Bahnasa lies on the edge of the western desert. "All the supreme prophets crossed through here. Can you imagine that? No other place in the world had this privilege."

El-Bahnasa was the Oxyrhynchus of Greek antiquity, and all the two British scholars excavating there in 1898 had to do was ask an Abd el-Razik about the papyrus texts they had discovered, for they could trace their ancestry back to Hassan ibn Thabet, the Prophet's poet, who was married to the sister of his Coptic Egyptian wife, Maria. They surely knew this land best.

"Our cousins flocked to this area for the corn, the maize, the cotton, the hay," Abd el-Razik explained. "Cotton was the most popular crop, the one that gave the best profits. They worked on a large scale." It also was close to the Ibrahimiya—the 250-kilometer-long canal built by the Khedive Ismail. "And then there was the railway line which ran just outside," Abd el-Razik added.

The Abd el-Raziks were originally judges. One, named Ahmad, had come from the Maghreb to El-Bahnasa where he ruled as Qadi al-Quda', "judge of judges," over Middle Egypt. The position was hereditary, and the family's sons customarily earned their diplomas in Istanbul. On his return from Turkey, Ahmad found his old friend Said Pasha installed as the new viceroy. "As in any house of princes, or presidents, there were intrigues. Some were jealous of Ahmad, and convinced Said to turn against him," explained Abd el-Razik. "Said did not receive him well, and he was poisoned."

Back on the farm, Ahmad's eldest son—also named Ahmad—and his closest relatives "chose four *feddans* and enclosed them behind stone walls to make the area self-sufficient," Abd el-Razik recounted. "There they built four houses for the married cousins and brothers, and a guest house."

The family houses are plain and identical. But the guest house! What was a *salamlik* with European flair doing so far from Cairo in the 1850s? Bordering the sandy lane to the residence were towering *Ficus nitida*, their green cube-shaped tops creating a stately first impression, as did a gigantic Indian rubber tree. The *salamlik* did not disappoint with its Renaissance pediments and windows, and wide wooden verandas with painted ceilings. One veranda faced east, overlooking lawns and flowering jacarandas.

Towering ficus trees that line each side of the entranceway to the *salamlik* have had their trunks washed in white lime, as do those seen in the south of France and in parts of Italy.

The large, gnarled roots of the orange-red blooming Flamboyant tree, first discovered in Madagascar in the 1830s, cling to the side of the entrance portico that has for its floor tiles decorative ceramics from France.

OPPOSITE
The *salon arabe* of the *salamlik* is one of several rooms extending off an octagonal central hall— an arrangement that could easily have been planned by a Frenchman familiar with the layout of pavilions like the Bagatelle just outside of Paris.

Much of the credit for the success of the plantation belonged to a "cousin," Zaki Pasha. "In spite of his ignorance, he was a genius," Abd el-Razik exclaimed. "He would change horses three times a day, and knew every meter of land from Beni Mazar down to Matai. He invented a seedless local fruit which they still call *keshta* Abd el-Razik."

Zaki Pasha also knew enough to plan a self-sufficient compound of buildings distributed in the Turkish style. The family's mosque was only steps away, and close by, the *madyafa*, or "office" for farm workers and villagers. The "guest house" served as common (though exclusively male) ground, where cousins and brothers gathered for luncheon every day.

"The eldest cousin would distribute the work between them, and tell everyone where to go next, whether Bahnasa or somewhere else," Abd el-Razik recalled. "There was no way they would have divided the land up. . . . It was a joint venture. They worked together. And they were very good together. They knew agriculture."

Presumably it was the Italian artists who struck a fanciful note to this dining room ceiling by including in the woodwork and arabesques the images of a quartered watermelon with a knife and fork—which was appropriate in a country known for this summertime fruit.

The *salamik's* central hall with its nineteenth-century European décor and framed verses from the Koran received Egypt's rulers, such as the Khedive Abbas Hilmi II, as well as cousins who lived a short walk away, among them, the erudite Sheikh Mustapha of Al-Azhar, mentor to modern novelist Naguib Mahfouz, and his brother Ali Pasha, known for his important treatises on Islam.

MOHAMED AMIN WALI HOUSE

El-Nazla, Faiyoum. 1860s

H igher and higher they went—and not only to see the skylarks, or catch the cool breezes after sunset. Nine children meant Hoda Zenaib needed a second story, and even a third, added to the old stone house in El-Nazla. "She shared in every decision. It was a partnership. And she even had her own property," recalled her youngest son Maher. Both his mother, and his father, Mohamed Amin, had come from the same village in the west of Faiyoum.

The farmhouse rising out of a thicket of date palms and shady semi-tropical greenery had been built in the 1860s by Maher's great-great-grandfather, Moussa Bey. It was more than just a holiday retreat for the children. It was headquarters of the family's *daira*—the management office of its agricultural estate that over the years had fluctuated in size like the idiosyncratic topography of Faiyoum's landscape and the shoreline of Lake Qarun. In the middle of the nineteenth century Moussa Bey had become a sizeable landowner as *sanjak*, or administrator, of the Khedive Ismail's domain of forty thousand *feddans* in the west Faiyoum. But the ruler who would accumulate more property for himself than any of his predecessors or successors eventually went bankrupt. And Moussa's support of the revolutionary officer Orabi meant his lands were sequestered. Yet his title of *wali*, or "governor," of the west Faiyoum had the luck to live on through his son Mustapha. He would found the Wali branch of this family of Hejazi origin, a Bedouin subtribe that had settled in the Faiyoum seven centuries earlier.

Mustapha was compensated for his father's loss thanks to the help of his former law school classmate, governor of Faiyoum, and later prime minister, Adli Pasha Yakan. The sixteen thousand *feddans* in the desert that he received would form the nucleus of the family's country estate, the *ezbet* Wali. The next step was to create buildings around the family's home for the guards and workers necessary to run the family farming operation.

The economic climate had been bad, and financing the irrigation canal proved uphill work. Nevertheless, the family was soon to plant sixteen hundred *feddans* of cotton, wheat, and *barsoum*, and acquire property in the provincial capital city. As a result, ever since Moussa's day, the *salamlik*, or reception room, at one corner of the house has seen a succession of meetings with tenants, workers, and other locals.

"My father Mohamed was a lawyer and judge before he was elected first to the senate, and then to parliament," Maher continued. He had taken over from Mustapha, adding on more houses, stables, and gardens behind low stone walls. "My father put in electricity in 1930," Maher added. "We had a special generator. It was a big advance for the time to have electric lamps."

"Of course some changes were made in the house. It was very old but we tried to keep as it was," Maher recalled. "We still had a cell for criminals, and a big kitchen out back." During Ramadan, "if anyone was hungry, they could eat for free," he added.

An arched stone gateway like this one belongs to the Egyptian countryside of the mid-nineteenth century. It delineated the area around the domain's residence apart from the adjoining agricultural fields.

A plaque outside the Wali house indicates that this is not only a residence but the *daira*, or "office," of the family's farming estate, which at one time spanned across thousands of *feddans* in western Faiyoum.

A balustrade staircase leads to the family's private quarters, as well as the room to one side that served as *salamlik*, or public greeting hall.

OPPOSITE
Egyptian country houses usually had a special room called the *salamlik*, which was designated for the men to receive their guests and hold local meetings.

The family mosque, built in a material from pharaonic times known for its hardness, remained intact nearby.

And how did his mother, Hoda, manage with all those children? "Of course we had nurses, maids, cooks, and drivers," her son confided. The *salon arabe* was furnished with canapés in the French style, while the big hall had a circular sofa and round chairs. Hoda, born in 1900, was one of the first ladies from Faiyoum to go to school in Cairo, where she had acquired a cosmopolitan taste. Maher also made the journey to the big city, but managed to remain close to the earth in his own way—with a career that brought him to the rank of dean of agriculture at the university of Al-Azhar.

L'HÔTEL SAINT-MAURICE

Giza. 1872–79

hat was a young French count with a great collection to do? It was March of 1871, and the khedive's circular had announced that "productions of the Islamic period were not free for commerce or exportation." The count of Saint-Maurice could only think to rush out and build a house in the center of modern Cairo. For the Khedive Ismail was handing out land in his new quarter of Ismailia to anyone erecting a house of value. The entrepreneurs had jumped in fast to profit from the promotion, but their stucco villas and Italian extravaganzas were not for a nobleman enamored of the glory of Mameluke sultans and Ottoman emirs. Only a town house in the *style arabe* would do for the count of Saint-Maurice.

The idea of salvaging Islamic artifacts had struck Saint-Maurice while out on horseback in the oldest quarters of the city, where he found himself side-stepping the remnants of ruined houses and collapsing mosques. Eager to clear the way for new boulevards in the image of Baron Haussmann's Paris, the road builders had plowed right through ancient lanes and pathways, leaving original Islamic decorations scattered about for anyone who wanted them. Nothing was too large or too small for the count to cart off in between the pack animals and pedestrians—from great medieval ceilings of stuccoed *muqaranas* to inlaid wooden doors, lace-like windows and screens of *mashrabiya*, marble mosaics, and ceramic tiles. He surely had learned to recognize more than just a good horse when he saw one!

Charles-Gaston Esmangard de Bournonville, to give him his full name, appointed the khedive's Master of the Horse in 1868 at age thirty-seven, had also been quick to provide Ismail with the regalia necessary for his new tree-lined avenues and formal gardens. To his English carriages with their liveried grooms, he had added Normandy horses, French postilions, and sixty magnificent carriages from Louis-Napoleon's private stock in Paris. He surely had learned well from Monsieur Fleury, the grand equerry who had made the French emperor's stables world famous with the credo that money did not matter: it was what money could buy that counted most.

In this grandiose frame of mind, Saint-Maurice set out to build a small palace that ended up costing him more time and money than he had bargained for. Completed in 1879 with a Mameluke façade of alternating courses of red and buff masonry and fleur-de-lis crenellations, the count's house also reflected the tastes of his architect Ambroise Baudry. The brother of the celebrated artist Paul who had come to Egypt in 1871 after German guns had rolled into Paris to interrupt his work on Garnier's new opera house would make his own Ismailia residence a veritable museum of Islamic art.

Even before its completion, Saint-Maurice's house was described by French journalist Gabriel Charmes as "a masterpiece of Arabic restoration." Standing in his salon, the count could look up to fourteenth-century woodwork from the *qa'a-s*, or noble rooms, of bygone houses joined into a vast ceiling spanning across to side wings, or *iwans*, lacquered in gold, and decorated with eight-pointed stars. A spectacular cupola scattered light from its *shamsiyat* or stucco grille-windows, set with colored glass.

Both exterior and interior decorations from the original town house of the count of Saint-Maurice were transferred and remounted into a replica designed in 1937 by Georges Parq and Jacques Hardy. Both of these Frenchmen were then working, and often together, in Egypt.

The architects Parq and Hardy reintegrated for their embassy of France a polychrome marble fountain, Andalusian arches, Roman columns, a carved wooden doorway, and Turkish ceramic tiles from Saint-Maurice's original patio.

Recovered from Saint-Maurice's town house were wooden doors with carved pentagons and hexagons and inlaid with pieces of ivory; panels of Kufic inscriptions, the earliest of Arabic styles; and stucco grille-windows, or *shamsiyat*, which traced back in origin to Damascus, and, in Egypt, were inspired by the stained-glass windows of ancient Coptic churches.

Behind Baudry's designs lurked the shadow of the greatest of Mameluke rulers, and the longest reigning, the Sultan Qaitbay. The late-fifteenth-century "prince of builders" had taken Islamic decorative arts to their zenith, and the best example of his extraordinary fine taste still stood, beside the Al-Azhar mosque. Here, in the sultan's *wekala* or "caravansary," built in 1477 to house traveling merchants and their goods, Saint-Maurice would find his greatest inspiration.

Inside, the count re-created Qaitbay's sense of somber quiet and beauty by replicating exquisite panels of polychrome marble for wainscoting and floors. Outside, a terrace boasted walls of transparent alabaster slabs, blue faience, and wooden screens. Broad palm fronds fanned out along the edges, and Roman columns and Andalusian arches stood to one side. By 1882, the count could recline on the tasseled coverlet of a chaise longue near a *fisqiya*, a basin of ancient marble mosaic. In his riding breeches and boots, his chest ablaze with medals, and wearing a fez, he cut a figure worthy of someone who knew him by name, Marcel Proust.

Yet, in truth, Saint-Maurice was deep in debt to his banker. And the Khedive Ismail was faring worse: his free-spending ways had cost him his throne, and the British had arrived to stay for some time. Even Baudry had gone—in a dispute over the high percentage of his honorarium, perhaps—leaving Saint-Maurice's house to be finished by his two young assistants. The count soon thereafter sold his house to the French government, and sent some two hundred pieces of his collection to the South Kensington Museum in London. Then, in 1937, like the ancient houses from which the count had drawn his richest furnishings, it too was demolished, and the French erected a new legation on the opposite bank of the Nile, taking the surviving gems of his collection with them. Saint-Maurice himself had disappeared, retiring, it was said, to the French countryside.

For this spectacular cut and carved cupola of the great center hall, the Italian decorator Augusto Cesari reinterpreted the one he had seen at the eighteenth-century Musafirkhana palace near Al-Azhar, where the Khedive Ismail was born.

The fifteenth-century Sultan Qaitbay consolidated the Mameluke style into a rich yet refined look that was typified by a sheathing of beautiful colored marbles for wainscoting and floors.

THE RESIDENCY: "BAYT AL-LURD"

Garden City, Cairo. 1892–94

C hurchill watched the dramatic battles of Africa from the comfort of High Commissioner Miles Lampson's vacated bedroom with air-conditioning—if he was not meeting downstairs with the generals Alexander and Montgomery, Anthony Eden, or Charles de Gaulle. On less pressing occasions, the Sahib Mustapha al-Demerdash Pasha, the best-dressed Egyptian in Egypt, and perhaps the richest, rolled up the front circular drive to sweep out of his latest model Renault in an exquisite striped-silk caftan, blushing peach *abaya*, and dress boots. And the aged Russian Countess della Sala, a glittering fixture of local society best remembered by an observant Harry Boyle for her hair "towering behind her like that of an El Greco seraph," still could make it up the broad front steps without much help before the arrival of Noel Coward and Cecil Beaton, and the inimitable Freya Stark.

Yet Regina Victoria was the one who counted most. For Queen Victoria's initials "RV" glistened in the morning sun out on the front gates. Few also could forget that "Bayt Al-Lurd"—the House of the Lord—was built to accommodate the living and working habits of Her Majesty's irascible consul general, Major Evelyn Baring, known as Lord Cromer.

Lord Cromer had arrived in 1883 to virtually take over Ottoman Egypt, then under British military occupation. His aloof and autocratic temperament often made him the subject of hearty local ridicule—especially after he strutted out the back doors and past the lawns and Lady Cromer's rose gardens to meet with his brilliant but eccentric secretary, Harry Boyle. Descended from a family of German bankers, the forty-one-year-old Cromer first sent to rescue Egypt's finances after his restructuring of British India, was not a man to joke with.

A need for more and better space than he had in the center of the city had sent "The Lord" scouting for property closer to the Nile. There he found a large tract of land inside a huge walled park that still contained the old Turkish saray of the late Queen Mother and a palace belonging to the wife of the reigning khedive, the Kasr el-Doubara. The "String Palace" would give its name to the new residential neighborhood and Lord Cromer's future letterhead, a name he likely did not realize referred to a Mameluke building technique known as *ablaq*, in which alternating courses of black and white stone were measured out by the length of a string.

Al-Lurd asked the Foreign Office in London to instruct its surveyor to draw up plans for the new offices and residence. The result was a handsome house with front columns and broad verandas on two stories in both front and back. All looked well before state affairs distracted Lord Cromer from noticing that the building had gone up with little attention to the prevailing winds, leaving him and Boyle to sweat it out in offices with full southwestern exposures. Even so, "the new Agency was more commodious than the former house and the social functions were on a more important scale," declared society observer Mabel Caillard. Here, too, Lord Cromer could test his legendary epicurean repertoire, which included prawn curry

The lawn rolled down to the water's edge, where the British government at one time had permitted Thomas Cook's travel organization to moor its Nile steamboats.

and reindeer tongues with peach bitters. Luncheon was served daily by his Indian servants in white turbans and gold-embroidered breast plates in a formal, portrait-lined dining room across the corridor from his office.

"The Cromers entertained extremely well," Mabel Caillard proclaimed, in spite of the unbending character of The Lord himself, who disliked the social functions attached to his position. "Everyone voted them a frightful bore but would have risked his or her life to be present." The great dances started after supper and continued on into early morning before Lord Cromer at last would approach his guests and ask, "Going?"

Sir Eldon Gorst's arrival in 1907 with seventy servants was only to be upstaged four years later by an imperious second Al-Lurd, General Horatio Herbert Kitchener. The legendary "K of K" had become a household word as Sirdar Field Marshal of the Egyptian army, avenger of General Gordon in the Sudan, and commander-in-chief of the army in British India. Here also was a man who liked to talk to his friends about art and archaeology when not tending to his gardens.

Who but "K" would drag along to his new home on the Nile his own bound volumes of *Country Life*? Kitchener lost no time in tossing out the yellow and chocolate canvases at the entrance doors and replacing them with hangings in scarlet and gold. His dinners were served on gold plate, raising more than a few eyebrows, and he spiffed up the unfurnished ballroom for state receptions, adding gilded cornices, Chippendale mirrors, and panels of brocades. He also ordered a new ballroom for a separate building to the north of the house, with the first sprung floor in Africa.

The Residency of the British ambassador was built like Whitehall and other government buildings of the day and furnished by the office of Public Works in London with both original and reproduced pieces, among them, Chippendale bookcases and William and Mary tables.

No matter who was visiting, Kitchener's redecorating projects took precedence. Even a prime minister come to discuss a crisis would first be asked to pitch in and help him move a heavy console! "Field-Marshals are, as a class, accustomed to swift, unquestioning obedience," noted his Oriental Secretary Ronald Storrs. And, at least twice a week Kitchener returned to the Agency from the bazaars and antique shops with almost child-like glee to undo his parcels and seek the approval of one or more of his staff. Even the pair of marble lions at the entrance to his residence had been wrestled away from the Khedive Ismail's former palace on Gezira Island and its Swiss manager. "Tales were circulated of the coercive methods to which he had been known to resort so as to induce the owner of some coveted object to part with his treasure," said Mrs. Caillard. "Agents all over the country were on the look-out for interesting pieces."

Kitchener, with his battle scars, glass eye, and a broken hip badly treated in India, was trusted implicitly by the fellaheen, however. "He is our master," one native remarked. Indeed, he would make his debut at Kasr el-Doubara to find its garden packed with petitioners. So respectful was the Bedouin sheikh El-Masri from Minya that Kitchener led him inside to a seat in his office on a winged leather armchair. As one native reportedly put it, "Every Egyptian had the feeling that the great Mohamed Ali had come back again."

Lord Cromer's office and study includes his Edwardian satinwood desk and his portrait by Sargent, which was once exhibited at the Royal Academy of Arts in London.

FATIMA HANEM CHAHIN HOUSE

Kasr el-Doubara, Cairo. 1890s

Whether chic Egyptian princesses or elegant wives of other diplomats, the ladies looked forward to Thursday afternoons when Fatima Hanem was receiving "at home." For her tea-time gatherings around the corner from the foreign ministry sometimes lasted into supper, when they would be joined by her husband and his colleagues from work. "We chose this house because of its proximity to foreign affairs, which made it practical for entertaining," Mahmoud Sabit Pasha told his descendants.

All of twenty-two back in 1918, Fatima Hanem, as ladies of quality were addressed in Turkish, was arranging her wedding trousseau with her mother when a Greek merchant put his 1890s mansion up for sale. Fatima and her future husband had gone to look for a house in Garden City, but it was this one in nearby Kasr el-Doubara, with "rooms that opened out one into another," that appealed to the pasha, who was master of ceremonies for Sultan Hussein and chamberlain to King Fuad.

Entertaining indeed became the hallmark of Fatima's mansion. Greeting her ladies were tall Nubian *suffragi* in white gloves and caftans of midnight-blue edged in gold embroidery. The Nubians cut striking figures in an enfilade of Louis XVI salons that took on a subtle air of upper-class London after the couple's return from a three-year posting there in the 1920s. With his smart mustache, British tweeds, and pipe, the pasha had attended an English boarding school before going on to Cambridge. Perhaps that was why, in this house where alcohol was never served, hidden behind the covers of two volumes of *Ecclesiastical Law* in his library was a bottle and six tumblers. The pasha liked "a spoonful of whiskey now and then," he explained, "for his health."

Shuttling across the pale Aubussons that Fatima had bought after the first war, the *suffragi* carried huge Christofle trays ordered by catalogue from Paris. They offered Fatima's ladies Lipton tea, cream cheese and cucumber sandwiches, tiny brioches, and English cake prepared by a cook and two assistants working in one vast kitchen in the basement. "We had Greek and Bulgarian maids upstairs," the Egyptian ambassador to Teheran and later Athens also was known to remark.

Dressed in high heels, pearls, and often, in Maison Worth, with red lips and nails, the chestnut-haired "Tamtam" did everything perfectly. She spoke beautiful French to her family and closest friends, among them Lady Audrey James, Mrs. Marshal Field after her liaison with Edward Prince of Wales was over, and Princess Eleana, sister of King Carol of Romania. Hating pretension, Fatima played down her husband's illustrious ancestry, which traced back to Caucasian tribal chieftains. Once allied with Tartar khans, they had adopted the traditional Mongol insignia—three horse tails, with an iron bar above, denoting "protection." To have the *suffragi* wear the tribal emblem, the *damgha*, definitely did not suit Fatima Hanem's tastes.

Before the men arrived, the ladies talked about the things that ladies enjoy talking about—children, fashion, and scandals. Only among her closest relations did Fatima speak of her own family—especially of a certain Greek lady who, in

Fatima Hanem's wooden wall-paneling came from Maison Kriéger, the Paris decorator and furniture manufacturer, which in 1904 began servicing clients in Egypt to compete with the rival house of Jansen.

Some of the town house's furnishings were acquired by Fatima Hanem's husband at local auctions; an amateur artist himself, many of his own works are seen on the walls. The portrait on the far wall is of Fatima's great-grandfather, Soliman Pasha.

1825, had left her husband to run off with a commander on a naval campaign in the Morea. Her lover was none other than Fatima's maternal great-grandfather, Soliman Pasha el-Faransawy, otherwise known as Abu el-Nizam, father of the modern Egyptian army. A French soldier of the Napoleonic Wars, he had come East to seek his fortune after Waterloo, and had converted to Islam. A photograph taken of him by the great Nadar hung in the main hallway. Fatima had heard many stories about him from her maternal grandmother, Nazli Hanem, his eldest daughter, who had grown up in his huge Ottoman palace complex in Misr al-Qadîma, Old Cairo.

Fatima liked to show her guests a huge portrait of Nazli's husband, Mohamed Sherif Pasha. Well-known for the superb cut of his French-made suits, and for his passion for shooting quail, Sherif had married Nazli Hanem after serving as a military adjutant to her father. Four times prime minister, and Abu el-Dustur, "father of the constitution," he had accumulated a vast estate in return for his services: twenty-five-hundred *feddans* in the Delta's rich cotton-growing provinces of Gharbiya and Sharqiya, nine *shoonahs*, or warehouses, in the port of Alexandria, and a grand Italianate palace designed by Franz Pasha in the residential quarter named after the khedive, Ismailia. Sherif also bought additional Sharqiya lands in his wife's name, "for safekeeping." For he shared the Circassian Mameluke conviction that a state is unlikely to seize land belonging to a lady.

Fatima had received the benefit of the land in her mother's name by way of a *hogga*, or will, through a *waqf* or trust set up by her grandmother to "protect her girls," one of whom was her mother, Gulsen Hanem. After Sherif Pasha had died in 1887, his eldest son was entitled to inherit two-thirds of his estate under Islamic *shari'a* laws. However, having fallen into the arms of a seductive Corsican adventuress in Paris, he mortgaged the entirety of his inherited lands in order to pay for his wife's expenses.

Nazli, at age eighty, set out to recover the land from his widow with a style that would have startled a Mameluke warrior. She named her daughters as life-time beneficiaries not only of her Sharkiya lands, but also of a choice property on the Nile's west bank in Cairo, later to be named after her—"Agouza," or "Old Lady." At stake also was the big Sherif Pasha palace in what by then was the busy commercial center of the capital. By the time Fatima was engaged and searching for a town-house, her father had died. So her mother simply swapped the Sherif palace out of one waqf and into another, replacing it in part—on paper that is—with the mansion in Kasr el-Doubara for Fatima and her husband.

OPPOSITE
A portrait of Sherif Pasha to the far left depicts the minister of the Khedive Ismail in formal attire and wearing his honorary decorations from the French, Italians, and Ottoman Turks.

THE WINTER PALACE

Luxor. 1907

"Have you heard the latest?" exclaimed an old aide-de-camp to Lord Carnarvon. "A wire came last night from the minister forbidding the visit of the ladies today." The head of antiquities Pierre Lacau "was wringing his hands and beard to me up to 12:30 last night, 'My God, my God, what to do! I don't know what H. C.'s action will be. Very likely he'll start filling in the tomb at once.' "

In his three-piece suit, bow-tie, and Homburg hat, with walking-stick in hand, Howard Carter had crossed the Nile from the West Bank early that morning on the thirteenth of February 1924. Once inside the sprawling Winter Palace just south of Luxor temple, he was "fuming, and pacing nervously up and down my room," recalled Charles Breasted, who was staying in the hotel with his father, James, the American pioneer in Egyptology. Soon anyone who was anyone in the world of archaeology in Egypt had also trickled into Breasted's room. For the fracas over Carter and his showing of King Tutankhamen's tomb to the wives of his colleagues capped a season of disputes and only disguised the real issue: The Egyptian government wanted Carter to renounce any claim to the objects he had found in the pharaoh's death chamber—and it was planning new and restrictive rules that were retroactive to his and everyone else's expedition in Egypt.

Carter blurted out one acerbic statement after another, "each one, as his anger ebbed, a shade less vitriolic than its predecessor," the junior Breasted later recalled. Only after his father came in from his bedroom next door was the British field archaeologist Carter mollified into posting a notice on the hotel bulletin board that ended with the words, "the tomb will be closed, and no further work can be carried out."

It was just one more unpredictable day at the Winter Palace, the majestic hotel across the Nile from the Theban necropolis. The hotel's affable Swiss manager, Anton Badrutt, known as "Toni," had grown used to the idea that anything was possible once the dramatic news of Carter's discovery had been broken to the world on the bulletin board in his front hall. The uncovering of King Tut's tomb also had been a great moment for Charles Baehler, the Swiss "hotel king of Egypt," who had hired Toni to run his Upper Egyptian Hotels group. But Badrutt now had to contend with the mercurial Carter and his equally volatile colleagues, whom he had no way of second-guessing. "Archaeology under the limelight is a new and rather bewildering experience for most of us," Carter later was to concede. Few knew what that meant better than Toni.

The son of Caspar Badrutt, who had opened the world's first "palace" hotel in St. Moritz in 1896, Toni had needed all of his previous training in London, Paris, and New York to cope with the onslaught of celebrities, royals, aristocrats, and countless others, including an aggressive world press, which, in Carter's own words, "the tomb drew like a magnet." Even without "Tut fever," the dusty-pink hotel with the pharaonic details on its broad façade attracted everyone who had made travel to Upper Egypt so glamorous in the 1890s. Set on twelve acres of grounds, the hotel that could sleep two hundred in grand style had replaced the fabled Shepheard's in Cairo as the jewel in Baehler's crown.

Drawing from his studies and work in Brussels, the Dutch architect Leon Stienon gave an Art Moderne veneer to his pharaonic motifs decorating the façade of the Winter Palace; G. Garozzo & Sons, one of Egypt's most active firms, built the riverside hotel on foundations by G. Siacci, inventor of a technique of building with concrete that carries his name, and which also was used in Cairo for the Khedivial Buildings.

One of Egypt's leading architects and son of a stonemason, the Dutch architect Leon Stienon designed the Winter Palace with a great main hall at the center of two side wings, and with an exterior staircase both in the front and back—an arrangement that he had perfected in his contribution to a number of buildings, including the San Stefano Hotel and Casino in Alexandria, which belonged to the same group of owners as this Luxor hotel.

OPPOSITE
The architect Leon Stienon brought to the inside of the Winter Palace the same motif of the sun and rays he had used outside on its façade; the great central hall's staircase was worked in wrought-iron and in the genre of Art Nouveau's "whiplash" technique that was fashionable at that time.

"A huge outstretched horseshoe terrace built on colonnades makes a welcome lounge overlooking the Nile, where steamers have their moorings, and double marble staircases lead to the entrance-hall," announced the *Egyptian Gazette* in late December 1906 as the hotel approached completion. The Dutch architect Leon Stienon had relied on his classical training at the Académie Royal des Beaux-Arts in Brussels, and eight years of practice in that city, when he designed a building worthy of the ancient glory of Luxor ("palaces") and the host of royal visitors to come.

The warm, sunny days of early February were high season for visiting the ancient sites, and the hotel in the tiny hamlet of Luxor was, as the *Gazette* proclaimed in 1923, "one of the most delectable spots in the world." Most guests ignored the warnings of French writer Pierre Loti, who sniped that the Winter Palace "dominates the whole town, and may be seen five or six miles away, a hasty modern production . . . a sham, made of plaster and mud, on a framework of iron . . . twice or three times as high as the admirable pharaonic temple. One such thing . . . is sufficient to disfigure pitiably the whole of the surroundings. The old Arab town, with its little white houses, its minarets, and its palm-trees, might as well not exist."

Hardly. This was not the "Poor Luxor!" inundated by "millionnaire daughters of Chicago merchants . . . with Baedekers in their hands, the same world that frequents Nice and the Riviera." This instead was a return in some measure to ancient Thebes, which had not seen such excitement since the Eighteenth Dynasty!

Indeed, the calm, colonial atmosphere of slowly revolving ceiling fans and Maple and Co. cushioned settees and lounges was rudely disrupted once King Tut's tomb revealed its golden treasures. Almost daily, the press had backed Lord Carnarvon into a corner of the hotel lobby, blocking him from its great staircase, and leaving him to escape up to his suite by a side elevator. Even the billiards and bar room on the ground level offered no peace from reporters—or from Carnarvon's collaborators, whose differences frequently had needed smoothing out by their expedition's patron before his unfortunate and untimely death from a mosquito bite.

Among the original areas of the Winter Palace were rooms for drawing, music, reading, writing, and smoking, as well as a billiards hall, with a bar and containing three tables, two English and one French.

OPPOSITE
The Winter Palace's original twelve acres of flower beds, croquet lawns, tennis courts, and kitchen gardens were contiguous with the grounds of the older Luxor Hotel that had been remodeled with Egyptian and pharaonic motifs; both establishments at one time were under the management of hotel proprietor Monsieur Pagnon.

The long, wide corridors and airy halls of the Winter Palace crawled with people, as did Carter's own "castle" on the hill across the Nile, and the Metropolitan House, the Ritz of the "dig-houses" for field archaeologists, just south of the Carnarvon concession. Carter's right-hand man, Alfred C. Mace, lent to the project by the Metropolitan Museum in New York, wrote to his wife from his room, "No one talks of anything but the tomb."

Any anxiety the VIPs might have had about seeing Carter open the tomb's sealed doorway after thirty-three centuries of closure were swept away once Toni's hotel staff arrived at the site. They came prepared with a five-star mid-afternoon spread of fish and meats, fresh fruits and vegetables, and chilled champagne, all transported over to the West Bank by boat, donkeys and camels. Only a few hours later Badrutt would turn out an equally lavish buffet for the Egyptian prime minister and a hundred and sixty guests back in the hotel's dining hall. With its big picture windows overlooking the Nile and its English fireplaces offering a welcome relief from any chill in the winter night air, the elegant hall also featured a regular nightly dinner *à la Tut* with a special menu card drawn up by Tony Binder, an Austrian illustrator and well-known photographer of Egyptian antiquities.

In the arcade of shops beneath the raised hotel terrace, visitors could pick up helmets, fans and "fly-flaps," film and postcards, and even antiquities—either real, or partly, or totally, fake. Meanwhile, back toward the gardens, sufficiently removed from the "store rooms and wine cellars," according to the *Gazette*, "capacious enough to stand a siege," were the kitchens, butchers' shops, vegetable stalls, and refrigerators, as well as quarters for the maids and valets of guests who still traveled with their servants. Here, too, the Breasted father and son had their rooms, which soon "became the clearing house for most of the complications and difficulties" that began to overtake Carter and his beloved Tut—whose tomb remained closed until the following season. Only after conceding his rights was the tomb in the Valley of the Kings handed back to Carter in late January 1925 "with great pomp," he reported to Lady Carnarvon.

MONTAZA PALACE AND SALAMLIK

Alexandria. 1892; and additions thereafter

A ll it took was a chance encounter—and one long look, in the lobby of the Grand Hotel in Paris, to reignite memories of the nervous splendor of Vienna on the spot for both of them. She dropped the bundle of roses in her arms, having just come in from the flower market at La Madeleine. He smiled and said, with characteristic aplomb, "The roses in Egypt are more beautiful." Much of course had changed since they had seen each other last. The young and irresistibly charming Prince Abbas had been fetched back from his studies in the Austrian capital in 1892 at the death of his father. He now had a wife, and four young children. He also was the khedive of Egypt.

Yet beneath the glowing chandeliers of the Grand Hotel in June of 1900, his grayish-blue eyes still had their magic sparkle. And Abbas Hilmi II, who had become khedive at just eighteen, still felt at ease around the beautiful and intelligent Hungarian Countess May Török von Szendrö. They had met when he was at the Theresianum, the elite academy in Vienna that had educated imperial Habsburg princes, European aristocrats, and Ottoman nobility since the eighteenth century. Among his closest school chums had been the brother of the countess born in Philadelphia and raised in Wassen castle near Graz.

The surprise encounter in Paris led to a long romance, and the countess became Abbas's second wife, embracing Islam as Djavidan Hanem. The secret marriage, in advance of an official religious ceremony in 1910, was lovingly contracted, it was said, in the romantic setting of Abbas's favorite domain—his seaside enclosure at *Montaza*.

It had been in the course of a promenade along the sea-swept coast to the east of Alexandria that the young Abbas had discovered and bought a small pavilion on a promontory jutting into the Mediterranean. He had wanted a home near the sea for the spring and autumn seasons he had so enjoyed in the forests around Vienna. With an Ottoman's love of gardening, he had accumulated huge tracts of desert for a park and gardens, and planted nearly half of the area with Aleppo pines. Marching down to sheltered rocky coves, cliffs and sandy beaches, the pines broke the force of coastal winds to allow him and his family and friends the pleasure of a daily promenade, a *montaza*.

Court architect Ernesto Verrucci sent the *quattrocento* soaring at the seaside domain of Montaza in 1924 by building a great *haramlik*, or family residence, for King Fuad, with an aerial tower to be seen from afar at sea—as one imagined the Pharos lighthouse of antiquity.

"I began modestly by buying a few sand dunes," the young sovereign later recalled. "I brought the water of the Nile, and immediately, the sand, transformed into soil, became fruitful, and trees and flowers sprang up. Then, little by little, I added and added, until now I have created quite an estate, consisting today of four hundred *feddans*." The sand had turned into vast date groves, wide lawns, avenues bound by orange trees and flower beds, nurseries for apricot and peach trees, botanical gardens—and some twenty-five miles of paved roads and pathways. Abbas even put in a private rail line and a small locomotive, which he drove himself back and forth to his official palace at Ras el-Tin.

At first the grandson of the Khedive Ismail had built only a small palace for himself in the Byzantine style. "Later I had a second palace built for my family in a veritable oasis," he noted in French, though he could have been as easily speaking in

English, German, Turkish, or Arabic. It was to be an oriental Mediterranean fortress, a honeymoon of Byzantine with neo-Gothic towers—hardly a cozy seaside getaway. Yet, for Abbas, his palace domain was a very secluded sanctuary indeed.

The surrounding grounds were soon filled with summer houses, grottos, banks of wild flowers, and a creek. Further on, rabbit hutches, a huge dovecot, plantations of fir trees, and a small park with fifty thousand mulberry bushes gave way to huge agricultural farms and stables, an engine-house for electricity, even a private telegraph and telephone office.

Abbas Hilmi II had built his Montaza retreat bit by bit, initially employing his father's court architect Fabricius Pasha for a pseudo-Byzantine palace in the likeness of his *saray*, or palace complex, for the family nearby. Fabricius, a native of the Aegean island of Syros who was of German origin, was soon replaced by the khedive's own architect, Antonio Lasciac, who, it seems, gave him a *salamlik*, or public reception house, in the style of an Austrian hunting-lodge.

Here Abbas also built an Austrian hunting lodge, as if to transport himself back to the Vienna Woods. A broad terrace overlooked the sea, but the front façade and its high roof and turrets benefited from a southern exposure that brought light and warmth in winter. Here also the khedive could survey his maps and railroading and agricultural plans and look over his long tables filled with reports. The simple, clean walls of a dining room suggested the latest work of the Viennese secessionists, while a small table under an Art Nouveau bow window was perfect for intimate repasts.

On the eve of World War I the romantic dreams of the 1890s were abruptly shattered. Disappointed by her husband's change of heart, Djavidan Hanem filed for divorce. As war broke out, the British crown claimed Egypt as a protectorate and deposed the vacationing Abbas as khedive. By 1924, his uncle, as King Fuad I, began to rebuild the *haramlik* in the Renaissance style of Siena—courtesy of his court architect, Ernesto Verrucci. The Mediterranean summer palace became a coastal castle, its lofty turrets and towers visible from a distance by land or sea. But the *salamlik* remained, commemorating sweethearts living out their dreams of the Vienna Woods.

Abbas Hilmi II likely first used this room with wooden paneling and alabaster columns as his office to hold meetings and go over his maps and plans for embellishing his Montaza domain.

The *salamlik* at Montaza was up to date with the latest trends that saw stained glasswork worked in what the Italians called *stile Liberty*.

THE CATARACT

Aswan. 1899

It was all very good news indeed for Albert Frederick Pagnon. The perfect Frenchman with looks, taste, and savoir faire, Monsieur Pagnon knew hotels the way the Thomas Cooks did travel. And he was not waiting around for an Anglo-French treaty to take hold of Europe. By 1891 the former Cook's agent had discovered everything he needed from the *Egyptian Gazette*: the French Riviera was empty for the winter season, while Cairo's hotels were over-booked and hiring out Cook's luxury Nile steamers to handle the overflow.

Next season Monsieur Pagnon moved into action. Back in ancient Thebes, he added an annex named the Karnak Hotel to his recently expanded and redecorated Hotel Luxor. A reputation for good food had caused his popularity to soar, and a stream of celebrities was soon lured to venture beyond Cairo to dine with Monsieur Pagnon as well as to see the ancient ruins of the upper Nile.

Monsieur Pagnon next followed Cook's holiday cruisers farther upstream to the tiny frontier town of Aswan. With Cook's backing, he built a comfortable but understated Grand Hotel near the landing-stage. But in 1898, as the first railway service had started, and Field Marshall Lord Kitchener returned triumphant from Khartoum to put in botanical starters on a small green islet in the middle of the river, the fifty-one-year-old Pagnon knew his time had come. Announcements for "Pagnon's Hotels on the Nile" suddenly included a new jewel to rival the finest vacation palaces of Cairo and Alexandria.

Just across the water from Elephantine Island was the picturesque village the ancient Egyptians called Shellâl, or "cascades," once a market for exotic goods brought by the great African caravans. A small bazaar still offered visitors the last crocodiles of Egypt. But most of all for Monsieur Pagnon, here was the terminus for Cook's steamers. It also was the point where the mighty Nile narrowed between big black cliffs and golden desert sand to create one of the most breathtaking scenes in Egypt. It was the perfect place for "The Cataract."

The first of the six great cataracts that are scattered along the river between Aswan and Khartoum would disappear once the British engineers inaugurated their High Dam in December 1902. "But nevertheless Cook and Son—a business concern glossed over with poetry, as all the world knows," opined French traveler Julian Viaud, writing in 1907 under the pseudonym Pierre Loti, "have endeavored to perpetuate the memory of the cataract by giving its name to a hotel of five hundred rooms . . . opposite the rocks—now reduced to silence—over which the old Nile used to seethe for so many centuries. 'Cataract Hotel'— that gives the illusion still, does it not? And looks remarkably well at the head of a sheet of notepaper."

Monsieur Pagnon was not one to take such acerbic remarks too seriously. Granted, his new *palais moderne* was not exactly a chateau, but rather a good sandstone building in handsome Mayfair white just above an outcrop of pinkish-red rocks tumbling down into the water and a small felucca landing-dock. Mayfair white on the Nubian frontier? Perhaps not for

Architect Henri Favarger of London designed this dining hall in the Moorish style after creating a similar room for Ethel Locke-King and her Mena House hotel at the foot of the Pyramids in Giza.

The Cataract's main reception area once saw Monsieur Pagnon directing his guests to daytime activities that included "paper chases" on donkeys and camels, as well as evenings of concerts, balls, and bridge parties.

OPPOSITE
Soaring Moorish arches, exotic lanterns, inlaid oriental furniture and *mashrabiya* screens grace the halls and salons of the hotel built by Monsieur Pagnon, who well understood that his guests came to Egypt not for Paris but to see Arabian nights.

OVERLEAF LEFT
French writer Pierre Loti saw the Cataract's dining hall soon after its opening in 1902 and likened it to one of the mosques of Istanbul.

OVERLEAF RIGHT
The hotel's upper-floor terrace offers views of the distant hills and the island of Elephantine in the middle of a Nile river that before the High Dam once ran rapidly over a solid barrier of granite, which then was broken into rocks of all sizes and shapes to create a cataract with treacherous cascades, whirlpools, and eddies.

Monsieur Pagnon. Rather it was more a matter of streamlined classical Art Deco, with two neat stories spreading their wings across the steep eastern banks of the Nile.

The original sixty rooms doubled the following season, and tents were needed out back to handle the crowd a year thereafter. Monsieur Pagnon soon was advertising large reception rooms, a billiards room, wide halls with fireplaces, a reading room with bookcases of first editions, and bathrooms big enough for small tea parties. This was a "house replete with every modern comfort" to keep his Anglo-Saxon guests happy, including the conveniences of pure water, sanitation, and "electric lighting throughout the night."

As Victorian as the hotel might have seemed in style and spirit, even the French backed down upon entering inside. For the hotel's décor largely belonged to the Arabic East—with horseshoe archways, wooden *mashrabiya* screens, ceramic tiles, chairs and tables inlaid with ivory and mother-of-pearl, and tambours. All of it was "perfectly furnished," the French traveler A. B. de Guerville reported, noting that it was all likewise "admirably looked after by M. Pagnon." An immense dining room built for the inauguration of the new High Dam in a separate hall that looked like a mosque also offered "a certain cachet of Islam," Pierre Loti remarked.

Few could argue about the food, which was "very good, very abundant," according to de Guerville, calling the service "absolutely irreproachable." What a review! Nubian servers in long white robes with red sashes, serving roast beef, plum pudding, and mince pies for the year-end holidays! "It is understandable the enormous difficulties that one needs to surmount . . . to offer daily, at six hundred miles from Cairo, a varied and excellent menu worthy of any of the big Paris restaurants, to hundreds of guests with appetites whetted by an open-air life. It is truly marvelous to find at the frontier of Nubia and at a reasonable price, all the comforts and luxuries to which we are accustomed."

In the end Monsieur Pagnon proved himself a great hotelier and was held in esteem as much as any of the Cook's. He would pass away at his beloved Cataract, of pneumonia, of all things, in 1909, shortly after retiring. The local paper called him the "Hotel King of Upper Egypt."

EL-MASRI PASHA SALAMLIK

Maghagha, province of Minya. 1895–1905

The men, women, and children had moved eastward across the Libyan desert in early summer, moving on horseback at night and camping by day. They had taken the southern route to avoid the soldiers on the beaches in the north. Reaching the frontier at Kufra, they followed their leader into Egypt, and a few weeks later would be staked down to the west of Maghagha. At last, they were free of the Ottoman *wali* Karamanli, his taxes, his cannons, and his bad manners! Only months earlier the Bedouin sheiks invited to the governor's palace in Benghazi had been massacred to a man. Luckily, their own leader, Keshar, had stayed at home.

Reminiscing about his great-grandfather, El-Masri Pasha sank into his chair and readjusted his gold-framed spectacles. In his flowing white robes and snowy short-clipped beard, he looked the picture of nobility as he thought about Keshar leading his tribe of twenty thousand Fawayid across the Western Desert in 1818. Because of his courage, El-Masri now had his country estate in Minya, his political clout, and a share in the Bank Misr that he had co-founded.

In three short generations the Bedouins had become rich and powerful landowners and builders of great houses! Could their ancestors, who had migrated to Libya from Al-Andalus ever have imagined this? It had been the *wali* Mohamed Ali Pasha himself who had persuaded Keshar to settle in Middle Egypt, granting him land in return for help in protecting his borders. His son and successor, Omar, would be first of the tribe to leave behind his tent for a house.

It had not all gone smoothly. El-Masri recalled the day he had rushed into a tent and the safety of his mother's arms as a child, after seeing his father El-Sa'idi shot dead by the viceroy Said Pasha's troops—by mistake, they claimed. His mother had hurriedly taken him and his two brothers, and sisters, back home to Suluk near Benghazi only to return many years later in the reign of a conciliatory but bankrupt Khedive Ismail.

Ismail's fall would be their gain. For agricultural Minya was the center of the khedive's *daira* and its hundreds of thousands of *feddans* of state and private lands sold to cover his debts—and bought by the likes of El-Masri and his brothers Lamlum and Mohamed. The brothers soon had their own sizeable *daira* of some eleven thousand *feddans* planted with cash crops of wheat, corn, and cotton. They also took pride in the silhouette of Kasr Lamlum rising up at the edge of the Western Desert, its parade of domes known as the "the white cliffs of Maghagha."

"The Libyans," as they were called, would not lose their Maghrebi accent. But they considered themselves as Egyptian as any native, and in 1882 had supported the military officer Orabi in his rebellion against Turkish favoritism in the army. A bundle of gold would bring them forgiveness from the British powers who had put down the insurrection; and an agriculture crisis reversed after European capital came pouring into Egypt for everything from railways to irrigation works. The boom was on, as well as the Belle Époque in Minya.

The main columned hall of the *salamlik* is dominated by a portrait of the pasha said to have been painted by an Italian artist in 1895.

At first glance, El-Masri's seemed like a modest farmhouse fronted by a small courtyard. But here was an Ottoman *salamlik* of the first order, flanked by a *madyafa*, or guesthouse room, with a nice exterior wall of woodwork and window panes to give it the name *oda izaaz*, or "glass room." A plain building, the *maktab*, or office, near the front gate, was restricted to meetings with farm workers and local constituents, while the family itself lived in a one-story *haramlik* some twenty meters away and set amid two *feddans* of oranges, mangoes, and grapes. The kitchen and storage areas were out back in yet another building.

Perfect for a Middle Egypt lifestyle and impressive to visitors were the *salamlik's* high airy ceilings and Tuscan arches and columns. They owed themselves to the Cairo atelier of the Jacovelli brothers, from Bari, no less. Nicola had apprenticed with the renowned *ébéniste* Giuseppe Parvis and his sons, and both he and his brother Giuseppe were being sought out by notables, including the khedivial family, top businessmen, even Lord Cromer and his British diplomatic agency.

The Jacovellis worked in a range of styles. But it was their restoration of Cairo's ancient mosques around 1890 that had convinced El-Masri to hire them for a *salon arabe* with all the flourishes. The brothers added geometric designs to big wooden doors, keyhole openings on French windows and doors, flowing Arabic inscriptions on upper wall friezes, and pierced-metal lanterns. The embossed velvet drapery and fine European furniture bought in Cairo had come from France.

The Bedouins had indeed arrived.

A running frieze of Arabic inscriptions added to the Jacovelli's decoration of this *salon arabe* for El-Masri Pasha.

The *madyafa*, or reception office, which flanked one side of the *salamlik's* front courtyard, was called the "glass room" because of its façade of glazed windows that had the markings of the Jacovelli brothers in Cairo.

Like most Egyptian country houses of the day, El-Masri Pasha's *salamlik* was built in 1895 with only one floor; the second level was added a decade later.

BINDERNAGEL VILLA

Alexandria. 1900–07

W hat could have happened to sting this German's civic pride so badly? Heinrich Bindernagel was a serious man. A rich and respected cotton merchant from Frankfurt, he had resided in Alexandria for many years, and was married to the daughter of the city's leading German importer. His life was German in every traditional sense. But he was also committed to rediscovering and preserving Alexandria's glorious past; and seeing his adopted city systematically uprooted by modern construction did not make him happy.

The Graeco-Roman museum had opened only a year earlier when Herr Bindernagel helped found the Archaeological Society of Alexandria in 1894. As its vice-president, he had supported the society's publication of scholarly bulletins to educate people about archaeology, and discourage them from clandestine excavations. It was thus fitting that bulletin editor Giuseppe Botti, the first curator of the museum, would dedicate his February 1899 issue to Bindernagel, while reporting on his own work at the site of the Serapeion, near the local landmark known as "Pompey's Pillar." There, the Italian archaeologist and his team had found a shaft leading to the temple of Serapis—a divinity created by Ptolemy the First to combine the Greek god Zeus with the Egyptian Amon-Ra. The new god took the form of the sacred Apis bull of the Pharaohs to become Osiris Apis or Oserapis, and thus, Serapis.

Botti's discovery in 1895 of a beautiful black granite Apis with a solar disk between its horns—carved during the reign of the Roman emperor Hadrian—had been a global sensation, attracting to the site some of the world's top experts. Bindernagel assured honorary memberships in the society for many of these visitors, among them, Professor Wilhelm Dörpfeld, who since 1887 had served as director of the German Archaeological Institute in Athens. Dörpfeld had also worked with Heinrich Schliemann in Troy, taking over the excavation there after Schliemann's death in 1890. Even more, he was a specialist in Greek architecture, and the companion in archaeology of the young man who had recently ascended the throne as Kaiser Wilhelm II.

Bindernagel would also sponsor many erudite publications about archaeology in German. But it was the appearance in Leipzig in 1900 of an altogether less scholarly tome, *Ramleh als Winteraufenhalt*—Ramleh as a Winter Resort—that would hit him like a bad storm. Suddenly, the demons of construction had invaded El-Raml (sand), the narrow strip of desert just outside the old city gates between the marshes and the Mediterranean sea. Everything appeared, from plain boxes in the dunes to English cottages and half-timbered Swiss chalets. What had become of the battleground where Octavian had dashed Mark Anthony and Cleopatra's dreams of a new Hellenistic empire in the East? Nothing remained of the once-sprawling Nicopolis that was Octavian's great commemorative "City of Victory"—except a crumbling temple on a cliff, and a few fragments scattered along the sandy shoreline.

Wilhelm Dörpfeld drew up informal designs for this villa based on the east portico and the porch of the caryatids of the Erechtheion, the fifth-century temple on the Acropolis in Athens which he was restoring, the most important monument of the Ionic style.

After the First World War, the Bindernagel villa was sold to the Lebanese cotton trader Georges Cordahy, known as the "king of the market," who retained its eclectic interior décor that included a *salon arabe* with carved woodwork and Turkish ceramics.

That was it! Herr Bindernagel decided to build a neoclassical villa on a high tract of land in Abou el-Nawatir (literally, "a source of water"), a district of orchards and kitchen gardens, plantations, and palms, and with a temple dedicated to Isis-Ceres, and overlooking the train station at what had once been Nicopolis. For its design, he turned to Professer Dörpfeld, who was working in Greece, at the newly rediscovered sanctuary of Olympia. Dörpfeld also had just begun to rebuild the Erechtheion, the most graceful temple on the Acropolis at Athens.

Before long, no passenger on the train could miss the columned Greek villa on the hill. At first glance, it might have been a cousin to the kaiser's own villa on Corfu. But on closer look, Bindernagel's villa was a neoclassical creation at its best, built to instruct rather than delight—a clear reflection of the Erechtheion. With its fluted columns and Ionic or ram's-head capitals, the villa seemed to celebrate the purity of the Athenians and ancient Attic myth.

Bindernagel thought a great deal about the gods of the Erechtheion: Athena, "defender of the citadel" and "Queen of Victory"; and Poseidon, with his trident and "salty sea well." Were these gods not also present in Alexandria? And had not the Ptolemaic Serapis, the principal god of Alexandria herself, the "goddess of the seas," also assumed the character of Poseidon? And what about Hephaistos, the matchless craftsman, and Boutes, the ploughman, worshiped for agriculture? Above all, the Porch of the Maidens with its caryatids, six statuesque girls standing as columns in their peplos gowns modeled on the local dress of the women of Karyai in Laconia: Were they not holding up the entablature with the strength and power of Rhine maidens? Wagner had yet to be understood at the Zizinia Theater in 1901, applauded by one journalist for "having had the courage to mount the *Walkyrie*." But what about Herr Bindernagel? Was he merely reveling in the delicious dreams of Hellenism, or was he using them to push forth the idea of a national soul?

Fortunately, his villa was far enough from the sea to escape the fiercely humid Mediterranean winds and allow use of the same Kara limestone from Mt. Hymettos that Dörpfeld had favored in his reconstruction on the Acropolis. But all the ideas of classical purity would fade once the Italian engineer and architect Aldo Marelli arrived on the scene in 1905. Marelli built a monumental center hall resembling a Roman atrium, with a great staircase and Carrara marble replicas of ancient sculptures of Venus, Diana, and Apollo. A *salon arabe* displayed Turkish ceramics and wall hangings, another showcased the Louis XVI style, and yet another was decorated in Art Deco. In a final statement of grandeur, an audience room off the entrance was mounted with a dais and readied with an enormous gilt-wood chair. Was Bindernagel expecting a god, a king, or a kaiser? Only the local Fates could truly know.

OPPOSITE
The building of the Bindernagel villa was executed by Italian engineer and architect Aldo Marelli, who also helped make this one of the finest neoclassical houses in the world.

This neoclassical villa reflected the tastes of Heinrich Bindernagel, who was passionate about archaeology, and had even patronized, with the city of Frankfurt, an expedition that discovered the lost city of St. Menas, the patron saint of ancient Christian Egypt. In his circle were not only Wilhelm Dörpfeld but other notable Germans: Professor Theodore Schreiber of Leipzig, expedition leader Ernst von Sieglin of Stuttgart, collector and philanthropist Wilhelm Pelizaeus, as well as Baron von Reinach, and Ludwig Borchardt, founder of the German Institute of Archaeology and author of the first intensive study of Egyptian architecture as a subject on its own.

OPPOSITE
"Herr Bindernagel had grown affluent and took on a certain regal grandeur," observed Mabel Caillard, who also noted that in his villa and off to one side of its great central hall was "a room with a dais, on which stood a chair so enormous and so golden only an emperor could have been expected to sit on it."

FAKHRY BEY ABD EL-NOUR VILLA

Girga, province of Sohag. 1902–06

The herald of Bliss arrived

Appearing early with success

The wealth palace was complete

With the Nile flowing by it

Joy called while writing history

At "Bliss" house is "Fakhry"

Poem by Sheikh Mohamed Salim laid into the foundation stone of the house

Fakhry Bey was just under thirty when Saad Pasha Zaghloul came to see him at home in Girga. So taken was the young Abd el-Nour by the pasha's presence that years later he recalled his visit as if it had been yesterday. "We used to hear a great deal about Saad," he wrote. "There was a lot of talk about him in the press. As we grew up, we always saw him in the public eye as an impressive figure." Saad, as the new minister of justice and future nationalist leader, was curious to meet a member of the old Coptic family from Upper Egypt; he had studied in Paris, and Fakhry's family had had long and close ties with France.

Fakhry offered his guest a high-backed gilded armchair made for the Khedive Abbas Hilmi, who, the year of his visit in 1909, had honored Fakhry with the Ottoman title of bey. "Tell me about his visit," Saad had asked. "The credit goes to His Excellency Boutros Ghali Pasha, the prime minister at the time," Fakhry replied. He then described how the villagers had gathered at the riverbank with flags, banners, and music to greet the khedive, following him from the landing stage up to the front gate.

Girga might still have been unpaved streets and open fields, but Fakhry's house had already become the talk of Cairo. What Abbas Hilmi was to see looked like the dream of an Italian nobleman lording it over a shoreline of date palms and tropical greenery. "Who built it? Did you?" Saad had asked, as he admired the spacious salons with tall French windows and balconies facing the Nile and the mountains beyond. "I told him I had inherited the land," Fakhry reported, adding that "the house had been built four years earlier," as part of his wife's wedding trousseau. It was constructed by a local contractor, El-Masawani, from the drawings of an Italian architect who had copied a palazzo on the Grand Canal in Venice.

The daughter of wealthy Coptic bankers, Fakhry's wife had been known for her grace and good taste. But her sudden death soon after their marriage had left Fakhry alone to handle his new house's interior decoration. Nothing in his dealings with agriculture, commerce, or banking had prepared him for the task of filling public reception halls at ground level and private quarters one floor higher. Fakhry's was to be a home where Italianate frescoes jostled with stained-glass windows, swags of Victorian drapery, and Second Empire furniture.

Indeed, the Second Empire look seemed perfectly worthy of a family whose land holdings extended as far as the ancient temples at Abydos and included eighty *feddans* in Girga and two thousand more nearby, planted with grain, orchards, flowers, and mint. Moreover, it had been back in 1869 that Fakhry's father, as consul of France in Girga, had hosted the Empress Eugénie as she was touring Upper Egypt in advance of the gala opening of the Suez Canal.

Fakhry's grandfather had had his own history with the French. El-Gladios, as he was called, was a merchant from Assiout, once the main trading center of Upper Egypt, and terminus of the Darb Al-Arbein, the "Forty Days Road" to the Sudan and the Western Desert. Heading south in 1798, El-Gladios had met some fellaheen who were frightened by a sighting of

This chintz drapery with its swags and jabots was original to a décor that greeted the visiting Khedive Abbas Hilmi II, whose portrait is displayed at center on the piano.

OPPOSITE
The villa, designed as an Italian palazzo, included classical elements as well as flourishes of the Art Nouveau style.

Bonaparte's General Desaix and his troops. As a Christian, he appealed to the French invaders and negotiated a settlement, which was accepted by the local Girgawi in order to keep the peace. After the French fled from Egypt the following year, El-Gladios was rewarded with land for his services. He in turn built a house and two mosques.

The foundation stone of the new house was laid at the far end of the family's domain, at the back of the gardens, where Fakhry's father had built a church to the Virgin Mary. The scholar and jurist Sheikh Mohamed Salim had penned a few lines on the occasion, calculating his rhymes so that the last verse brought the total to 1324, the date in the Arabic calendar when the house was completed. "Saad Pasha was very pleased with these verses," Fakhry remembered. "But then," he remarked, "isn't one meaning of the name Saad 'bliss,' or 'good luck'"?

ZAAFARAN PALACE

Ain Shams. 1902

Small and slight, but no longer the Circassian beauty in frilly European dresses and jewels, the second princess, Djananiar, usually sat in the same French armchair, wrapped in a roomy *meshlah*, her eyes hidden behind dark glasses. She still moved her hands gracefully, and wore a lovely Ottoman silk *hotoz* at a becoming angle, her hair streaked with a blaze of henna. A small folding table with cards for playing patience stood within reach, her cigarettes not far away. "I never actually saw her smile," her step-granddaughter, Emina Tugay, later recalled, "though she was amiable enough. As soon as my mother was announced," the third princess, Djechme Affet, "tall and forbidding," came in from her own suite of rooms across the great stair-hall, "dressed in the latest fashion, with her hair done in a brown pompadour."

Receiving only a privileged few, among them Emina and her mother, the daughter of their husband by his favorite and youngest concubine, the two old ladies were the last of the Khedive Ismail's harem—the last harem of Egypt. Called the second and third princesses by foreigners, these two of Ismail's four "official" wives had followed their husband into exile more than a decade earlier and had become good friends. After his death, they had returned, taking up residence together in the desert just outside Cairo, where they built a palace in the Art Nouveau style then fashionable in England and France. Here they continued to live in the same seclusion, with the same formal protocol that had ruled their entire adult lives. Presiding over their household of Circassian *kalfas* and other servants from Nubia and the Sudan was, in the tradition of earlier centuries, a chief eunuch.

For Emina, visiting them "always stirred in me a pleasurable excitement." Indeed, the princesses' palace was of a beauty and refinement unlike anything else in Egypt, with a feeling of lightness and space, romantic elegance, and gaiety, nestled inside a picturesque park of green lawns and flowering gardens with sandy yellow pathways. Indeed, the two *principessas*—long confined with their husband to a borrowed palazzo in Naples—were as au courant as any of their contemporaries in the West.

This was the second palace named after the once-vast neighboring fields of flowering violet-pink saffron. The first had been a modest getaway built by their husband in forty days and offered to his mother in 1871, and later to his favorite, Emina's grandmother. Throughout the new building, the widows memorialized their husband Ismail with the monogram "I" surmounted by a crown and a small crescent, encircled by a wreath of garlands and ribbons or flanked by decorative griffins. Breaking up the vast walls were gilded stars, palm fronds, and draping garlands, which for the princesses were redolent of the world of Marie Antoinette, if not Josephine. A modern elevator near their spectacular staircase was unique in the Middle East.

The princesses had found a kindred spirit in Cairo in the court architect, Antonio Lasciac. Summoned at one point to Istanbul by the young ruler Abbas Hilmi II, who summered on the upper Bosphorus like most of his family, the enterprising native Austrian and future Italian national had embraced the *stile Liberty* introduced into the imperial Ottoman court by his

The architect Antonio Lasciac added ornamental Art Nouveau touches to his Beaux-Arts palace for the Khedive Ismail's two widows, the last ladies of his harem, which was the last harem of Egypt.

A rich décor of draping garlands, Palladian arches, parquet floors, and Charles X furniture attested to the tastes of the princesses, who were familiar with the palaces and villas of France.

OPPOSITE
Designing with the fluid lines of the *stile Liberty*, architect Antonio Lasciac assured that the great wrought-iron staircase of the princesses' palace would be reputed the finest in the Middle East.

friend, architect Raimondo D'Aronco. Back in Cairo, Lasciac would add a cast-iron staircase to a pink marble palace for Said Halim Pasha, a would-be ruler of Egypt turned Ottoman Grand Vizier. Yet it was for the princesses that he reserved his true genius. For they too were au courant with the Liberty style's Near Eastern roots, which would ignite the fluid and sinuous lines of Art Nouveau to climax in Paris at the World Exposition of 1900.

Lasciac's exterior iron railings for doors and balconies were grounded in modern French tradition and heralded the curvilinear worked-iron forms to be found inside. At the foot of the dramatic sweep of broad steps leading to the private quarters, the Persian bird-beast *simurgh* stood guard in polished brass at each newel post, as if nesting on the Tree of Knowledge—an ancient motif not to be missed by the princesses, whose last days would be devoted to educating their late husband's youngest descendants.

At the far end of the building, potted plants and other greenery joined with high walls in trellis-work several years before Elsie de Wolfe would make them famous at the Colony Club in New York, recalling the palm courts of the great hotels of Europe. Rococo woodwork framed tall mirrors to further increase the opulent breadth of space, while a ceiling of sky blue with a whisper of floating white clouds had seemingly traveled from a small music room at Versailles. A huge rectangular skylight in yellow amber glass painted with delicate floral arrangements instantly recalls the casino at Vichy, not to mention La Bagatelle Gardens in Paris, and the delicate stucco-work of the Petit Trianon at Versailles. The last ladies of the harem had been kept out of sight, but traveling each summer in black silk mantles and white veils, they had seen it all.

MANIAL PALACE

Roda Island, Cairo. 1901–33

S o sorry to meet you in such chaos," Prince Mohamed Ali Tewfik told his guests one afternoon, greeting them in his house on Soliman Pasha Street with outstretched arms and a smile. "But I am leaving. I have sold my palace. For me the entire charm of the place was in this delicious garden with its high walls protecting one from prying eyes, at a time—it seems only like yesterday—when this quarter was free from these huge buildings. But today—Look!" He pointed up to the high apartment blocks towering over his garden. "In a few months' time this garden will be covered with houses. Confound this mania for building!"

The younger brother of the Khedive Abbas Hilmi II, the prince had traveled the world after going to school in Switzerland and attending the Theresianum in Vienna. Now with free time and a wide circle of friends, he wanted a home away from the noise and dust of modern Cairo. Of all the places the Khediva Emina, his mother, had suggested to him, it was fifteen acres of gardens that once belonged to his great-grandfather Ibrahim Pasha on the Nile island of Roda that suited him best. Here in 1901, at age twenty-six, he found the perfect spot to build a storybook *haramlik* with a high and fanciful tower for his library, with open views to the Citadel and the Pyramids back to the west. The prince would spend the next thirty years embellishing his island retreat and adding pavilions to its grounds. Naming his Turkish *saray* the Manial Palace, after a Mameluke emir once ensconced on this island, he also would devote himself to reviving the Islamic arts.

Inside the entrance gate, by the main door to his *salamlik*, the prince typically greeted his guests with old-fashioned Ottoman courtesy. "Dressed to the nines," his grandnephew Abbas Hilmi III recalled, "he wore his tarboosh at a debonair angle, and had the smell of eau de cologne." In his later years he sported a well-trimmed white beard, and always, his lucky emerald ring.

"He came because of the banyan trees," his grandnephew explained. The prince was struck by the sculpture-like offshoots of a huge Bengali ficus, a survivor from the days when the Bahri Mameluke sultans ruled their medieval empire from this island covered with orchards and pleasure gardens. The tree had also ignited the imagination of Ibrahim Pasha, whose passion for the plants of India would become legendary.

The prince was soon joining his gardeners in their search for rare botanical specimens. "He had traveled a lot—to Iran and Iraq, Syria and India, and even Zanzibar," his grandnephew remembered. "He had his agents looking all over"—not only for plants, but also for objets d'art. One of his agents was Gayer Anderson, the British major who would restore two seventeenth-century houses in Islamic Cairo.

Enclosed within high, stone walls, the prince's domain had a Moroccan lookout tower in the Rabat style to guard over it, and stables for his Arabian horses. A pavilion for his Golden Hall stood at the far end of the property, its spectacular gilded

Prince Mohamed Ali Tewfik said that his Manial *saray*, or palace complex, was built by him and the *moallem*, or master builder, Mohamed Afifi, whose name appears with his on the front gate. Yet stylistically it seems his brother's court architect, Antonio Lasciac, also might have added his ideas to the *haramlik*, which, in 1901, became the first building of the prince's domain.

The entrance door, sheathed in copper oxide and worked in the Mameluke style, announces, in Arabic, that this craftsmanship was *Misr Shoghl* —"Made in Egypt."

The essential courtyard of any Islamic house enters the prince's *haramlik* to dazzle its visitors with a spectacular double-height hall with an Andalusian marble fountain and a triumphal Moorish archway decorated with beautiful blue glazed tiles and monumental strokes of Thuluth calligraphy.

The *Shami*, or "Syrian" Hall, and its windows pay tribute to oriental gypsum dormers, or *shamsiyat*, and the art of colored glass that traces back to the great Umayyad mosque in Damascus. The exquisite *boiseries* here were rescued from a dilapidated palace of the powerful al-Azem family, governors of Damascus in the eighteenth century.

OPPOSITE
A small sitting room of the prince's *salamlik* testifies to the glory of rich craftsmanship. Here are wooden panels of ebony and sandalwood worked into rectangles, stars, and lozenges, lattice-like *mashrabiya* screens, and *kursi*, or hexagonal side tables, made in various hardwoods and covered with mosaics of ivory.

woodwork shipped from Istanbul and the *yali*, or grand waterside residence, of his maternal grandfather Ilhami Pasha, who had wed an Ottoman sultana. Another pavilion showcased the Regency Room that had the ceiling of its long main hall ornamented with a gilded sunburst, one of the oldest Ottoman motifs; its walls were lined with portraits of Egypt's rulers by the court painter, Heydayat. Here the prince also had reused his grandfather's old red-velvet drapes and gilded French armchairs, while on the floor above were his Aubusson carpets, period Louis XV furniture, and Sèvres porcelains. An Ottoman room with Turkish divans included his mother's four-poster rococo bed in solid silver, as well as a gilt baroque fireplace from her *yali* at Bebek on the European side of the Bosphorus. The fireplace did not keep him from "putting in central heating," noted his grandnephew. "He also was the first to have a Carrier air conditioner."

The *salamlik* included a Moroccan hall that displayed the colorful reds, browns and yellows of Andalusian wall tiles, with stained-glass windows, and antique Tabriz carpets; while the eighteenth-century boiseries from a crumbling palace that was among the many once belonging to the Al-Azem family, one of Syria's premier families, contributed to another. "The idea was to save things," the prince's grandnephew said. "He was interested in style. Some things were genuine. But if he couldn't have them, he would make them."

The prince patronized the Ilhami School for crafts-making in Cairo, a *waqf*, or religious trust, in memory of his maternal grandfather that produced objects of all sorts, even ivory fly-whisks. He "always meant the palace to be a museum where young people could come and learn," said his grandnephew. "If they could not travel, they could come here and see all the styles."

Mohammed Ali Tewfik welcomed to his Manial domain people with a variety of views—writers, poets, journalists. The French composer Camille Saint-Saëns stayed as a house guest near the banyan trees and played the second movement of his fifth ("Egyptian") piano concerto. "Churchill came to the blue salon during the war," noted the prince's grandnephew. Still, the prince "was very conscious of rules of protocol . . . and had a very strict way of doing things." There were tea parties in the gardens, fancy affairs with the diplomatic corps, and also "boring family occasions," revealed his grandnephew. "My father came once a week to see him when he was alone." The prince was not always alone, however. He had a French lady as his wife.

BARON EMPAIN PALACE

Heliopolis. Circa 1910–11

Sir Reginald Oakes, a civil engineer once employed in Brussels, was named president and general director. André Berthelot, head of the Paris Métro, was brought in to attract French financing. And cosigning as local partner was Boghos Nubar Pasha, the well-connected son of the once most powerful of Egypt's ministers. Everyone and everything was moving into place, just as Édouard Empain had wanted it in 1905, "for a corner of the desert where I have a certain interest."

The world's greatest specialist in transport and electricity had embarked on a new project unlike anything else he had ever before attempted. What had got into the greatest stickler for organizational details? It had to be more than bargain land prices and the fresh air that he hoped might cure his morbid fear of viruses. Whatever it was, it was enough for him to launch into motion the *système Empain*, with its network of banks and holding companies stretching from Sweden to South America.

At fifty-two, Empain stood not a hair above an inch and five feet. The son of a village school teacher, he had risen like a meteor in the universe of industrial development. Now he wanted to create a green oasis on a desert plateau northeast of Cairo. His aim was to re-create the ambience of the French Riviera, with a luxurious palace hotel to rival the casino at Monte Carlo, and, above all, a showplace villa for himself.

"It shall be called Heliopolis," he told the young Belgian architect Ernest Jaspar. Indeed, his City of the Sun was to rise up near the site identified by the Belgian archaeologist Jean Capart as the ancient locale sacred to the sun god Ra. "I want the architecture to conform to the tradition of the country," Empain went on. "You love the mosques; you are an architect. Why don't you submit a proposal?"

Eight days after visiting Empain's "corner of the desert," the twenty-seven-year-old Jaspar delivered his plans. "Go back to Europe," ordered Empain. "Get your family and return as soon as you can." For the baron's passion for technologies still fueled his legendary obsession with rapidity. His motto for success? "A fast decision, even if it's a bad decision, is always better than one that drags on."

In his dream of a satellite city reachable from the center of Cairo in a matter of minutes, Empain had caught the contagious aspirations of his sovereign, Leopold II, king of the Belgians. With his penetrating, blue-gray eyes and his clipped, authoritarian manner, Empain had proven himself Leopold's most loyal servant. No task had been too absurd, no caprice too extravagant, to fulfill for his "old master."

The Orléans side of Leopold would create Empain a baron, with a coronet of two lotuses to recall Egypt. Yet it was the cold-blooded Saxe-Coburg side of the Belgian king that would summon his subject to his every bold new adventure and make him risk his own capital in *terrae incognitae*. A childhood penchant for devouring atlases and maps had prepared Leopold for grabbing up distant lands of his own—even hoisting his colors on the banks of the Yellow River!

Rising from a high, artificial platform, Baron Empain's palace exhibits the same mountainous *shikhara*, or spire, with sister finials that seem to push each other heavenward, as in the glorious Hindu temples of Khajuraho in north-central India.

CLOCKWISE FROM TOP LEFT
Did French architect Alexandre Marcel transform a dwarf Vishnu from the sanctuaries of the Chandella kings into a sun god for Baron Empain?

Dazzling, and astounding in detail, the sinuous, twisting, and voluptuous figures of Baron Empain's palace are more restrained than the "rioting figures of love and lust" immortalized in the Khajuraho temples that had inspired his French architect Alexandre Marcel.

Like the Khajuraho shrines, a pillar of grotesque beasts is offset by elaborate horizontal friezes that often depict lotus flowers—in Eastern traditions the counterpart to the rose — and embellish a décor that seems to grow from the building itself.

The rich sculpture of the Khajuraho temples, praised as some of the best Hindu art in India, appears here in animal figures and even a Buddha; included also is the elephant, which in India is a symbol of moral strength and protection.

In 1901 Empain had begun laying rail lines across Leopold's newest private domain, the ivory-and-rubber-rich Congo. Only three short years earlier he had been in China, putting in a line of railroads, the backbone of an industrial power in the making. The king had no need to worry about cash flow with Empain around to handle his Société Asiatique and its complicated finances. Any problem could always be solved by his managing director at the Cairo branch of the Banque Sino-Belge. "From the start," Empain attested with tempered resignation, "he squeezed me like a lemon."

Leopold's energy would inspire Empain beyond his imagination. As builder of the Paris Métro, he had already shown courage by holding the line against the critics of Hector Guimard's subway entrances with their limply swaying Art Nouveau metalwork. He also had discovered the talents of the Orientalist architect Alexandre Marcel, who had designed an exotic Salle des Fêtes on the Left Bank in the Rue de Babylone, and, for the Exposition Universelle of 1900, a Khmer temple for a Cambodian pavilion, as well as an eclectic Panorama-du-Tour-du-Monde for the France/Extrême-Orient passenger steamship line.

Leopold was electrified by Marcel's Panorama, and asked him to replicate two sections of it—a Japanese tower and a Chinese pavilion—in Brussels. Seeing these, Empain signed up Marcel on the spot to build him a version of the third section of the work, a Hindu temple.

Just returned from India, where he was building an immense Italian neoclassical palace and a replica of the gardens at Versailles for the Maharaja of Kapurthala, the graduate of the Beaux-Arts school in Paris headed straight to Egypt. He arrived to find Empain reviving the forgotten beauties of Islamic art with Jaspar's help. Habib Ayrout, a local entrepreneur, had been hired to set things straight when the initial plans sent from Brussels did not work out. For, no matter how much oriental veneer was used to disguise a European distribution of spaces, the Egyptian climate required bigger balconies and terraces, and demanded that kitchens be located well away from front doors.

Empain at once gave Marcel carte blanche to design a number of palaces, one with Moorish arches and ceramic tile-work for his partner, Boghos Nubar Pasha, another for his childhood friend, the Prince (later Sultan) Hussein, and a third for Hussein's wife, the Sultana Malek, who soon saw herself residing under Moorish horseshoe arches, high crenellated terraces, and a dome like a mosque's.

Empain's own palace on the Avenue des Palais offered the same striking features that had thrilled the public at the Exposition. Marcel constructed an artificial elevation that gave Empain distant views of the pyramids on one side, and looked onto the basilica where he would be laid to rest on the other. Ascending terraces were planted with grass and furnished with an eclectic array of statuary, including graceful nymphs and an erotic marble statue of David. Still, it was the symphony of Far Eastern motifs and Hindu dancers that would make the heads of many celebrated visitors spin.

On trips to the Indian sub-continent, Marcel brought back seated Buddhas, Shivas, a flute-playing Krishna, and other avatars of Vishnu, complemented by assorted elephants, lions, peacocks, and twisting serpents. The individual pieces were cast in reinforced concrete, which had been pre-poured and molded using a system devised by the French inventor François Hennebique.

Inside, Marcel's collaborator Georges-Louis Claude unleashed his artistic fantasies, filling the ceilings with Chinese dragons and the same Hindu dancers he had created for the Panorama. It may have boasted Egypt's first elevator, but Empain's palace also gave Louis Seize full play in gilded doorways, Belgian mirrors, parquet floors, and Aubusson carpets.

The baron at last had his great new home.

The life of hunting, feasting, dancing, and music enters Baron Empain's palace, where among the upper wall decorations is the image of Krishna with a flute, the Hindu symbol of love.

Baron Empain's palace was one of the first in Egypt to install an elevator, which, along with a spiraling wooden staircase, led to a pillared outdoor theater on the roof level above.

YOUSSEF PASHA SOLIMAN VILLA

Abbasiya. 1914 and thereafter

It was Youssef Pasha's small *salamlik* that grabbed the attention of his honored guest, the visiting King Fuad. Added on right after the First World War, the guest house built by the Italians had started out as a garage for four cars, among them a black Renault for winter, and a cabriolet for summer, "a Benz, as they called them then," according to the pasha's grandson Mounir. "The Mercedes came with its own driver," he explained, "but he went back to Germany during the second war." Yet the short, stout king was not looking for cars as much as he was trying to decipher the Arabic calligraphy on a curious panel high up on the façade. To his surprise, the angular fourteenth-century Kufic style of writing was no familiar historic inscription. Instead it read: "In the name of the Father, the Son, and the Holy Spirit."

"You see," Mounir affirmed, "it was a time when the Islamic style was in fashion." The same Italians who had given Youssef Pasha's villa its good Palladian arches and columns with clean and elegant capitals could easily shift gears into the decorative language of the Mameluke sultans. For the delight of the eminent jurist, who was head of the Orthodox Coptic church's influential administrative council, they chiseled out a cornice of stalactites crowned by fleur-de-lys cresting like a row of dolls against an open sky. Inside, a great carved mahogany staircase competed for attention with walls of Turkish tiles, while a high dome studded with stars of colored glass towered over a marble *hammam*. "He had great personal style and taste," Mounir went on. "He was a very courageous man," piped in another grandson, also named Youssef. "He believed in freedom of expression in religion . . . from his heart."

The pasha considered Egyptians as one people. This thought no doubt had endeared him to a king ruling under British occupation. It also had appealed to his friend and former neighbor in north Cairo, the nationalist leader, Saad Pasha Zaghoul. In 1884, at the incredible age of only twenty-two, the pasha had been appointed attorney general of Cairo. He presided over many local high courts, as well as Egypt's exterritorial judiciaries, the Mixed Tribunals. He also was among "the first generation to speak Arabic without a Turkish accent," his grandson Youssef declared. "He knew French, had studied Italian, and Coptic," the language of Egypt's earliest Christians, which was mastered by few. He was elected a member of parliament, was named minister of agriculture and, later, of finance. "They chose him because of his sound legal judgment," his grandson stressed.

The Upper Egyptian from Minya who had grown up some kilometers north of Cairo in the small Delta village of Sindebis could now well afford to live like other professionals, out in the fresh air of Abbasiya, at the edge of the Suez desert. Originally a royal suburb founded by Abbas Hilmi I in 1848 on nothing but pure sand and Bedouin camps, as would want any ruler like him born in Jeddah, this area certainly offered more comfort and space. "We were the Zamalek of Cairo," volunteered Mounir, referring to the rich residential district to develop later on a lush green island in the Nile.

Angular Kufic calligraphy in the eleventh-century foliate style adorns the frieze on the main façade of Youssef Pasha's *salamlik*.

Stylistically, Youssef Pasha's villa on the street called Azim el-Dawla—a name derived from Turkish meaning "the great one of the nation"—resembles the work of Giuseppe Tavarelli, who at one time was chief architect of the technical division of the Ministry of Wakfs, or Islamic religious endowments. The Italian professor and architect also designed the Orthodox Coptic Cathedral when the pasha headed the church's administrative council.

The pasha's dream house had archways, columns, balconies and terraces, and gardens. "He had traveled a lot," recalled his grandson. "It was a necessity then to go to Europe, for culture more than for pleasure." He hired Italian stonecutters and carvers who copied the country villas they knew in Tuscany or around Rome. "You see, the king had grown up in Italy," Mounir explained. "We had Italians everywhere. The police spoke Italian; if you called on the telephone for information, even the operators talked Italian."

King Fuad had come to extend Easter greetings to the pasha and his house guests, the young crown prince and future emperor Haile Selassie of Ethiopia and his wife. Once past the entrance gate, the king could see stone-fruit trees, sandy pathways, two gazebos, and gardens planted with "one-offs probably picked up at the ministry," according to Mounir—everything from a khaki tree with a tomato-like fruit to a variety of mangoes and red dates. Originating from the pasha's orchards in the Delta was his "Soliman Pasha" orange, a cross between a Valencia and the local sour *baladi*. Tasting like a navel orange, but with a thinner skin, each piece was wrapped and sealed for export in fine paper with the label King Ramsis. "He was the first to send oranges abroad, and they were much appreciated by the Germans, especially the Kaiser," reported Mounir.

The pasha received the king inside his villa's *istekbal*, or foyer, which was open to his visitors and constituents on Saturday afternoons—the "common area of the house," as Youssef termed it. "Guests did not enter the house," the grandson added—not even the king, who was visiting on "official" business. The villa might look European, but it conformed to the Turkish tradition of rigorously separating public and familial spaces. Even the royal house guests had to go around back to reach the main entrance staircase, which led them to the *piano nobile* and their private apartments, just below those of the pasha and his family.

OPPOSITE
The central hall of the pasha's villa could accommodate reunions with important guests or family members. A suite of chairs is signed by Maison Kriéger of Paris, while bracketed, high-back chairs are examples of a type known in Egypt as *Assiouti*.

"He knew furniture," Mounir interjected knowingly, surveying the great center hall where the pasha's suites of fine French furniture in the Empire style took center stage over a no less handsome set of high-back armchairs from Assiout. A leather sofa and chairs signed by Paris furniture maker Kriéger gave the Pasha's library the requisite seriousness, while a parlor lined with Louis XVI replicas served to display the gifts newly received from his latest guests—a jewel-handled sword, a shield and spears, carpets of monkey skins, and the prestigious Order of the Star of Ethiopia. Other precious pieces were relegated to the dining room. "On his way back from Carlsbad each year," explained Mounir, "he brought lovely porcelains from Moser House, and glassware with his initials engraved in gold and with a cross and a crescent in the middle."

LOUTFY MANSOUR HOUSE

Alexandria, 1910s and later

N azli Hanem was firm in her decision. She would put her trust and faith in another man. Not that anything had gone wrong with her marriage. It was just that in 1952 her brilliant young husband had started his own family firm, the first in Egypt for exporting cotton, thus obliging them and their boys to move to Alexandria from Cairo. A former government regulator and cotton specialist who had studied agriculture at St. John's College in Cambridge, no less, Mahmoud Loutfy Mansour was so absorbed by his new venture that he had given his wife a free hand to do as she pleased with their new house in suburban Gianaclis.

Located near the swank San Stefano Hotel and Casino, the house was one of two nearly identical Italianate villas built in the 1910s by a Greek contractor. Nazli did not have to think twice about whom to call in to help with the decorating. With his tailored good looks, wonderful sense of humor, and excellent taste, Victor Lehmann was at her service. After all, he was Jansen's man in Egypt. "He was Jansen Egypt," Mrs. Mansour declared, speaking in French. And indeed, Lehmann was last in a line of branch managers for the famed Paris decorating house and furniture maker that had been favored by the rich and famous since the 1880s. With his spacious showroom on Sharia Fuad in Alexandria, and workshops both there and in Cairo, the Frenchman with German-Jewish roots was a legend. Arriving in 1939 at age forty or so, Lehmann had made a splashy debut by adapting Jansen's classy old-world European style to the needs of a newly arrived cotton mogul and press magnate, Oswald Finney. Lehmann would transform several floors of Finney's city center apartment building into a Renaissance palace of oak boiseries, rococo stuccowork, and terraces of European marble statuary.

His reputation was made. Europe might have been at war, but in Egypt there was no stopping the demand for Lehmann's custom-made versions of Louis XIV, XV, and XVI, even French Empire, Italian Rococo, Chippendale, and Queen Anne—and most of all, perhaps, the added touches of chinoiserie. It was all "style, style, style," proclaimed "Ali Lehmann," the decorator's right-hand man. What was good enough for the Alexandria governor's office or a new Arab League headquarters in Cairo was certainly good enough for Nazli. She took immediately to Lehmann's "ancien faransawi" look, with his preference for decorating with Gobelins and Aubussons. "The cache-pot in the living room weighed 300 pounds," she noted, adding that some of the objects had come from the houses of Sherif Sabri, which had been done up by none other than Jansen's top decorator in person, Stéphane Boudin. "The government was nationalizing, and people were unloading whatever they had," Nazli explained.

And that was how the Loutfy Mansours had come to buy the house of Madeleine Boudin Tadros, whose husband had been a lawyer for the Suez Canal. Madeleine had been famous for her large and beautiful garden, and had won awards for her arrangements of calla lilies, gladiolas, and birds of paradise. "She had brought some seeds from the Riviera," Nazli remembered, adding that after the revolution she had returned to buy back one of her Caucasian rugs in a local showroom. Nazli's house would be Lehmann's last in Egypt. With the revolution, it was time for him too to pack his bags and return to Paris.

Madeleine Tadros was "the queen of gardens," according to Nazli Hanem, who notes that her predecessor on Rue Nikitaides had created "the best-looking one of Alexandria," with walkways, statues, Roman marble benches, and bronzes of figures from Greek mythology. A figure of Apollo was only fitting for a house built by a Greek and offering views of the sea from its top floor. The gardeners were Egyptians.

RIGHT
Before departing from Egypt in 1956 as the last of several managers for Jansen, the esteemed Paris decorations house, Victor Lehmann operated a huge showroom on Sharia Fuad, where Nazli Hanem could easily obtain carpets, furniture, ceramics, and other accessories to fill the good-sized rooms of her early-twentieth-century house.

BOTTOM
To find a house with grounds near the sea had delighted a native of the south of France like Madeleine Boudin, who had originally lived here with her husband, Antoine Tadros. The second of two identical villas was rented to an emir of Mecca exiled by the Saudis.

OPPOSITE
Even decorator Victor Lehmann might have picked up decorating tips from Nazli Hanem, who best described her grandmother's impressive marble palace in Cairo, built by Italians in 1840, as having "nine gates, a thousand windows, curtains of pearls, thirty-eight doors, all in the Islamic style, and each with a different design . . . [with] wooden ceilings, domes with mosaics of colored glass, Arabic writing, ceramics . . . and six kitchens."

PRINCE YOUSSEF KAMAL HALL

Matariya. 1920s

H e came to them like Lorenzo the Magnificent, a prince who needed no crown, an artist in spirit and nature. He had sent for painters from Italy and France to teach them. "How great it was when he sat for us," one of the students later recalled. "He checked our work, and criticized us and the foreigners he had allowed in for the lessons. I remember there being an Italian painter. But the prince did not like his work much and joked with him: 'It seems to me as if you are painting an Italian.'"

In 1908, at age twenty, Prince Youssef Kamal had just become the richest member of his family. A sportsman since boyhood, he had taken up the arts and sciences with as much passion as he had horses and hunting—a tradition that had come down to him from his great-grandfather Ibrahim Pasha, and Abbas Hilmi I, whose name alone meant the world's greatest stud of Arabians. Now the prince had endowed a school on the French model in Cairo to teach Egyptian boys art and architecture. Some he sent to study in Paris, including one destined to become the country's most important sculptor, Mahmoud Mukhtar.

Later the prince would also serve on the Committee of the Conservation of Monuments of Arab Art, led by the Hungarian architect Max Herz Bey, and he amassed a collection of ancient maps, books, and objets d'art with the drive and discipline of a German. "They are the only serious ones!" he liked to say, speaking in any one of six languages, including Arabic, Persian, and Turkish. His humor was as legendary as his wealth—most of which he would give away to culture and charity.

The prince came into his fortune following his father's death in 1907. Yet it was not until after the First World War that he would build a residence at the edge of the desert northeast of Cairo. Here, in the ancient village of Matariya—"water of the sun" in the Coptic language—the prince would erect a structure that would more than make up for the small, modest villa nearby of his father, Egypt's biggest landowner, who had an important stud of Arabians and stable of carriage horses.

The prince sought out architect Antonio Lasciac, who had long served his cousin, the Khedive Abbas Hilmi II. After the signing of the post-war treaties, the Austrian national from Gorizia had returned to Egypt as an Italian! Working for the ruling family, as well as many upper-class Egyptians, Lasciac knew better than any that a princely household, even without wives and children—Youssef Kamal was to marry only briefly—needed a lot of space. His newest client required room to display his ancient Mediterranean maps (the finest then in private hands) and a great *Monumenta Cartographica* charting the deserts of Africa and Egypt. An entire room was turned into a maze of tall, narrow cabinets filled with thousands of books, many of them first editions, some of them penned by the prince himself, as well as a complete set of Napoleon's *Description of Egypt*.

The fact that the house stood in the middle of agricultural fields did not restrain Lasciac's ideas of princely splendor. The great hall fronted by royal palms looked like a Roman palace, with its monumental balcony and triumphal arcade seeming to await the arrival of some important leader. This was not the Lasciac of the Vienna Polytechnic, but an architect bred in the Italian capital city, where he had completed his studies and later would be elected to the Academy of San Luca.

Architect Antonio Lasciac perhaps was inspired by his palazzo for the Colonna family in Rome when he designed this "hall" in Matariya for the richest member of the Egyptian royal family, Prince Youssef Kamal; the residence of the great explorer and hunter who penned *Around Africa* in 1928 is now the Desert Research Institute.

Did Youssef Kamal secretly wish he was a prince of the past? His *salon arabe* with its polychrome marble fountain would have delighted the Sultan Qaitbay; while pleasing to any Persian or Ottoman ruler were walls sheathed in blue-green floral tiles and display cases filled with five hundred pieces of Iznik and Kütahya ware; while a Mameluke emir would have lauded a great astrolabe in brass, "magic balls," and metal incense burners, trays, and candlesticks, much of which are now in the Islamic Museum in Cairo.

A decorative wall unit in polychrome marble, alabaster, and gilt-work signals that both the prince's decorator Carlo Bugatti, who gave Moorish styles to European furniture (before his son started designing automobiles), and architect Antonio Lasciac could easily shift from Italian to Islamic styles; both the prince and Lasciac had served on the Comité de Conservation des Monuments de l'Art Arabe operating in Egypt from 1882 until the 1952 revolution.

Many of the prince's friends, such as the Esterhazys of Hungary, considered the hall at Matariya not to be forgotten for another reason: the prince was one of the world's greatest big-game hunters. His collection of trophies from the Rocky Mountains to the Himalayas made his entrance hall, with its great central staircase of polished red Aswan granite, look like a museum of natural history. Here were displayed every type of game: lions, tigers, panthers, and beasts with antlers of multiple points. Even a giraffe peered down from the main balcony.

Arriving for lunch at one or dinner at eight, his guests would find the prince at home in the style of a maharajah. A brilliant polo player, Youssef Kamal also had a hunting pack to rival any of the most prized Hungarian Vizlas, and demanded strict ceremony and dress of those invited to *la chasse* on his grounds.

The central hall was a gentleman's affair with leather couches for conversation with Turkish coffee. While there were a few European pictures, the prince's true taste was to be found in his oriental hall. There inlaid wooden doors, built-in sofas, and Turkish and Persian carpets competed for attention with the finest medieval enameled-glass lamps, metalwork, and ceramics by the hundreds. Vermillion reds and vibrant aqua blues shone from seventeenth-century Iznik jugs, ewers, and bowls, alongside eighteenth-century polychrome Turkish *qumqums*, dishes, jugs, and bottles. The seats were modern oriental-style divans that the prince had ordered custom-made from the Milan workshops of Carlo Bugatti, the designer of rich and exotic furniture and interiors, who had proven his skills in the Khedive Abbas Hilmi's palace in Istanbul.

It was also here, around a fountain of colored marbles, amid medieval *azulejos* imported from Spain, that the prince hosted his favorite evenings of oriental music and song.

A true sign of a prince and *grand seigneur* in Youssef Kamal's hall was the carved wooden cupola and drum above his *salon arabe*, which was decorated in the Islamic style—as was his entire house in Nag Hamadi on his sugar plantation of thirty thousand *feddans*; his seaside villa in Alexandria was sleek and modern.

PALAZZINA DR. ALI PASHA IBRAHIM

Garden City, Cairo. Circa 1922

E arly one morning, Dr. Ali Pasha Ibrahim passed an old man on a donkey on his way to work. The famous surgeon kept his eyes on the man as he continued walking, until finally he called for him to stop. *Aih ya raïs!* the doctor rang out. "How much for that carpet you're sitting on?" he asked. *Ya genieh ya basha*, replied the man, thinking he would make a killing by asking for one Egyptian pound. "That's not enough," the doctor shot back, "I'll give you five." Off jumped the man at lightning speed to hand over his saddle rug to Dr. Ali Pasha. *Mutashakereen awi ya basha.* "Thank you very much, pasha."

With no more than a quick glance, even from a distance, Dr. Ali Pasha Ibrahim could spot the right combination of color, texture, and form with near-scientific precision. The father of modern medicine in Egypt and a genius in the operating room, he had achieved the highest honors at the Royal College of Surgeons in London before being knighted by King George VI. The first Egyptian dean of the faculty of medicine at Cairo University—a post long held by his British colleagues—he also would head up the Egyptian Medical Society. But his greatest passions were music, photography, and literature, and, above all, collecting fine objets d'art.

Ali Pasha always declared that he owed everything to his mother. An illiterate but innately intelligent woman, she had gone against every Muslim code by divorcing her husband and sending her son to school in Cairo. He did not disappoint her, and excelled in everything, including sports. It had been his school field trips to the Citadel and its Mameluke palaces and mosques that had sparked his lifelong interest in art.

"He collected everything—pharaonic antiques, early Islamic and Greco-Roman antiquities, textiles, bronzes," noted his granddaughter, Professor Mona Serageldin. There were Persian ceramics, Mameluke metalwork, Chinese porcelains, Flemish paintings, and fine French furniture. Yet it was the priceless ceramics and precious oriental carpets for which Dr. Ali Pasha would be best known and admired. "He had two Islamic salons, one a study, the other where he received his guests," noted his granddaughter. Even before the second war, a visiting King Alfonso XIII of Spain had "asked to see the collection and came for a private tour."

But where could the busy doctor house himself and all of the objects of his desire? Luckily, the hospital and college of Kasr al-Aini had once been part of the palace of the Khedive Ismail's mother and the old *sarays* on the Nile belonging to his father, Ibrahim Pasha. In 1905 a group of Syrian-Lebanese developers had bought the queen mother's former backyard and its sinuous canals, which they transformed into the exclusive district of elegant villas and grounds known as Garden City. A lot at the juncture of two leafy, curved streets had caught the eye of the twenty-five-year-old student of medicine. But it would be another fifteen years before the space would be transformed by palms, acacias, and oleanders, a tennis court, a garage, a wooden oriental kiosk, and a marble Mameluke fountain.

With a porter at the front gate, and a garage around to the back on a side street, Dr. Ali Pasha Ibrahim had the privacy of a Garden City villa shaded by tall palms and flowering acacias, and grounds that included a pavilion designed with *mashrabiya* windows and "an authentic Mameluke fountain reassembled from numbered pieces," recalls the pasha's granddaughter Mona Serageldin.

The Tuscan *palazzina* designed by Giuseppe Tavarelli—an architect from Carrara and one-time professor at the Royal High Institute of Fine Arts in Rome—gave a good theatrical overcoat to the parquet floors, coffered ceilings, and ceramic-tiled walls inside. These owed themselves more to the son of Giuseppe Parvis, who had studied in Turin before taking over from his father, the doyen of oriental decoration and furniture-making in Cairo.

The Palladian arches, balconies, moldings, and classical draped garlands cloaking the exterior little prepared the visitor to be greeted inside by a pair of giant elephant tusks! Nor did one expect an exquisite eighteenth-century *chaise à porter*, or an English wall clock under the stairway set to chime precisely at six a.m. to signal the Nubian valet to bring the doctor's morning coffee. There was a French Gothic dining room, a salon in Louis XVI style, a music room in pure Empire. "The style was mixed. We were looking both to Istanbul and Europe," noted Mrs. Serageldin. "We wanted a Damascus in France."

Yet two Islamic salons were sheathed in floral ceramics from Asia Minor, with their vibrant greens and blues. Fatimid

The entrance hall with its gilt and coffered ceiling gave way to rooms that, according to the pasha's granddaughter, were "each designed in a different style"; staff rooms on the uppermost floor were "like dormitories, with tags on the door keys."

In devoting two small salons to decorative Islamic motifs, Dr. Ali Pasha Ibrahim was among "a group of Europeans and cosmopolitan locals who chose to decorate in the 'exotic' style," notes his granddaughter, Mona Serageldin.

Stained-glass windows added visual warmth to Dr. Ali Pasha Ibrahim's villa, where the dining room with a fireplace had been outfitted in the French Gothic style.

lusterware plates lined up inside one vitrine, while a medieval brass inkwell was to be found under a sixteenth-century Mameluke lantern. Nearby, an enormous Qalawan vase bore the four ducks of the Bahri Mameluke sultan.

And the carpets! Covering a grand divan and strewn across the floors were Bukhara carpets with rich, velvet pile. Elsewhere the visitor tripped over prayer rugs from Asia Minor, Transylvania, and west-central Anatolia, and bold seventeenth-century Ushaks. There were elegant and stylized floral Ghiordes, muted Bergamas, polygonals from Konya, floral borders from Ladik, and geometric patterns from the Caucasus. And the Safavid Persians could only be outdone by the distinctive red-and-black geometrics of the Samarkands.

Mrs. Serageldin counted ninety-four carpets. "They were huge, and couldn't all be displayed at the same time," she recalled. "The ceramics that were not in the vitrines were packed up, and the carpets rolled up in a special way. We had three big rooms down in the basement. The rooms smelt of moth balls and petroleum to keep away the mice."

MIZRAHI PASHA VILLA

Maadi. 1920s

E manuel Bey Mizrahi at first was too busy practicing law to give the idea serious thought. But as his firm handled the business affairs of King Fuad, and later those of his son and successor, Farouk, he often met up with other Jewish professionals connected to the Palace. Many of them belonged to Egypt's most elite families—the Cattauis, the Suares, the de Menaches, the Mosseris, and the Rolos. These families had built far-reaching empires in trading, finance, banking, railroads, and land development. Often educated abroad, with foreign titles and protection, they were rich, powerful, and sophisticated. And they loved to live in great houses.

So it seemed quite natural for Emanuel Bey to make his move when a consortium of these esteemed names joined forces with equivalent British interests to form the Delta Land and Investment Company in 1907. Their idea was to develop a new suburb to the south of Cairo, named for the *maadi*, or ferry-boats, that once plied the Nile between Cairo and Giza.

Some of these financiers had invested in a railroad line that bypassed the Maadi site on its way to the royal winter resort of Helwan. Fortunately, they also had bought land on either side of the tracks, and planned to invest in a new line linking Maadi directly to downtown Cairo. A dozen years after the first quarter-acre plots were laid out, the trees and lawns planted, and the streets paved, the design had succeeded beyond its developers' grandest expectations. Cairo now had its own British colonial haven.

Quiet, clean, and picturesque, Maadi attracted an array of international businessmen, diplomats, and even members of the Egyptian royal family. For everyone—including a group of Ashkenazi newcomers—it seemed the place to live. Almost the only people who did not want to move there were its mostly Sephardic investors, who preferred to remain in their fairytale mansions in Garden City, Kasr el-Doubara, and Giza.

Emanuel Bey, however, was in a class of his own. He was enchanted by the idea of living among Madagascar's flaming red poinciana trees, South American jacarandas, colorful, shady *lebbeks* and *tecomas*, casuarinas, and eucalyptus—not to forget Maadi's agricultural fields and orchards filled with apricots, guavas and mangoes, grapes, crab apples, and ground nuts. For Emanuel Bey, with his impeccable tailoring and sweep of distinguished gray-through-chestnut hair, loved nothing more than gardening. Perhaps it was his ancestry; the name Mizrahi—"oriental" or "sun rising"—had been brought to the region by the many Persian Jews who had settled in Turkey. And had not the Persians given the world some of its finest gardens?

Emanuel Bey bought four *feddans* only a stone's throw through the date palms and open fields from the exclusive Maadi Sporting Club. Before having to give up the sport because of his health, he often visited the club to play golf, at which he had become a champion. He built four large mansions on the corner of Mosseri square in the *mas provençale* style of southern France—one for him and his wife and two children to live in, the others to rent out. His tenants later included members of the

These royal Havana palms were as popular in the garden suburbs of both Cairo and Alexandria as they were in southern Florida or along the French Riviera and in Monaco.

Emanuel Mizrahi created a relaxed and comfortable atmosphere inside his Maadi house that in the aftermath of the revolution of 1952 became the residence of Mexico's ambassador to Egypt.

royal family, among them a princess married to an Anglophile sportsman, the first Egyptian member of the Gezira Club. Emanuel also would plant the town's largest and most exotic garden.

"It was enormous and elaborate," his granddaughter Injy declared. He put in his own nursery and a fern garden. His collection of cacti was said to rival even Prince Mohamed Ali Tewfik's most prized specimens at his Manial Palace domain. Emanuel also introduced to Egypt the bird of paradise, which was sent to him from South Africa in lieu of payment by a Cape Town client. "His favorite flower was a rose called Edith and Helen, a pink rose as big as a cabbage," his granddaughter reported.

A tiny wooden pavilion, "La Pachinette," at a far corner in the woods was built so his daughter could go there and paint. A bunker, hidden beneath the lawns and rocks, also had gone in during the war.

The house itself had a warm, family atmosphere, which suited Mizrahi's wife, a pianist, who led a very private life. But her husband was something else. "He was quite a prankster. Once he dragged a donkey into the grand living room where my grandmother was giving a concert," Injy recalled.

OPPOSITE
Emanuel Mizrahi, the last Jewish pasha of Egypt, built one of several Mediterranean houses around his gardens, the largest in the Cairo suburb of Maadi, which had been developed on the plan of Khartoum.

Emanuel Bey had attended law school in France, and was later awarded the highest honors by its government, including the Légion d'Honneur. He also was decorated with the Grand Cordon of Italy. His fame as a lawyer came with his help in drawing up the Montreux Agreement of 1937, which phased out the system of capitulations and the Mixed Courts that had long prevailed in Egypt for natives of the twelve European nations and those under their protection. He also had handled the Egyptian government's dealings with the Suez Canal Company. Taken together, his services were such as to have King Farouk elevate him to the dignity of "pasha."

He would be the last Jewish pasha of Egypt.

SINOUT BEY HANNA VILLA

Giza, Cairo. 1924

"What, me obey the order?" bellowed an impeccably tailored Sinout Bey Hanna. In spite of an official order to do so, the dark and slim Saeedi in his early forties was not one "to cease and desist" from criticizing the British powers and their chosen prince, who was now to reign as "sultan." His eyes ablaze, his tone of voice defiant, the feisty Upper Egyptian would plead his cause for independence in the local press—regardless of the consequences.

Yet by 1923 the crisis over Egyptian independence had ended. Sinout Bey had returned from exile in the Seychelles, and his hero, the nationalist leader Saad Pasha Zaghloul, was now prime minister under a new constitution. Even the most elegant ladies had thrown their veils to the wind, and a new green flag was hoisted up bearing both a cross and a crescent—symbols not seen together since Saladin's day.

This turn of events was a great personal triumph for Sinout Bey. One of Saad Pasha's most devoted supporters among Orthodox Copts, his convictions were such that even a French education by the Jesuits had done little to restrain him from polemics that had ignited the passions of a nation. Sinout's zeal had even caused him to be escorted from Cairo on more than one occasion. Yet, in the end, few could help but admire his courage. At one point he had even risked his own personal safety to defend the future prime minister, Mustapha Nahas Pasha, from a would-be assassin.

Who could find fault with this fastidious man who returned from the Indian Ocean with a carefully wrapped set of toilette articles in the most exquisite tortoise-shell? And who was not secretly amused by his habit of keeping his favorite white gloves unsoiled by opening doors with his elbow? The second son of first cousins from the provincial capital of Assiout was not an exclusively political animal: he loved to play cards for money at the Ramses Club, and to go hunting for objets d'art in Paris.

Joining Saad Pasha and his Wafd party at the Versailles Peace Conference after the war, Sinout found time for more than political maneuvering. He would dine on the Champs-Élysées before peeking in on the late-night cabarets, dragging along, in full Arab dress, a reluctant Hamid Pasha el-Basil, a Bedouin magnate from Faiyoum. In the morning Saad Pasha was always quick to ask his adorable trouble-shooter, "Where were you last night?"

Before the riverside road was added, the villa of Sinout Bey, which is now the residence of the French ambassador to Cairo, was like many of the first residences in Giza that faced north and had their grounds extending to the water's edge on the west bank of the Nile.

Sinout Bey had little time to answer, for he was rushing out before conference meetings to browse through Siegfried Bing's fashionable Maison de l'Art Nouveau for the most contemporary home decorations and accessories. He also needed to stop by the Galeries Lafayette, where Louis Marjorelle had created an Art Nouveau stir with a dynamic, free-form iron stair-railing. Another Marjorelle, Louise, from a family of silk manufacturers in Lyon, was his good friend, as was her husband and colleague at the Versailles talks, Wassef Pasha Boutros-Ghali.

Back in Cairo, the future five-time foreign minister Wassef Pasha had charged his wife, Louise, with finding a spot for them to build a house. To Louise, the lush west bank of the Nile was a perfect choice, not only for her and her husband, but

A columned gallery above
the entrance hall gives the
impression that this is still
the land of pharaohs and
ancient temples.

for Sinout, too. This still undeveloped area offered open views of the Citadel, as well as the Pyramids to the west. Its mature trees and other greenery were remnants of a huge park and botanical gardens put in for the Khedive Ismail half a century earlier by Jean-Pierre Barillet-Deschamps, the landscaper of Paris.

The sycamores and acacias reminded Sinout of his family's rambling villa in Assiout, and when Louise called in the Italian engineer Domenico Limongelli for herself, Sinout asked him to build something for him as well. By then Limongelli had become more than a construction engineer solving the problems posed by shifts in riverfront soil; he was becoming known more as an architect, and was a familiar figure in high social circles in both Paris and Constantinople after marrying the daughter of the influential Armenian minister, Artin Pasha.

Limongelli designed both villas in the Palladian style, reflecting his training at the Fine Arts Academy in Rome. At Sinout's house, the central hall rose two full levels to a huge rectangular skylight of stained glass above an elegant columned gallery. Below, colorful geometric carpets covered wooden parquet floors, and flanking the doorways were two pairs of gilded lamp-posts in the style called *Empire, retour d'Egypte*.

Easily seen through glazed French doors leading to a dining room were seen that essential attribute of Art Deco oriental luxury: a gold-lacquered mural on panels. This particular work, depicting exotic antelopes and gazelles, had been executed by the interior decorator Jean Dunand, whose lacquer screens and furniture graced the *Normandie*, called "the most beautiful ship afloat."

Sinout ultimately lost his house in a card game. Was this an end to his luck? Not so. While the house of Wassef Pasha and Louise was destined to be torn down, Sinout's survived in style, courtesy of his beloved French. They went on to buy it and make it the residence of their ambassador in Cairo.

OPPOSITE
French doors of glass, and
sleek, unadorned wall
surfaces set the tone for the
dining room's big lacquered
screen designed by Jean
Dunand, a disciple of
decorator Eileen Grey.

GREISS PALACE

Mîr, province of Assiout. 1922–24

Bishai Bey was not an especially devout Christian. Yet, the tall and dark *'omda*, or mayor, of Mîr dressed in the gallabiya of the fellaheen considered himself blessed. He believed, as did his villagers, and most everyone else around, that even the most unfortunate people became fortunate in Mîr. The reason? It went back to biblical times, when the Holy Family, in its sojourn in Egypt, had walked through Mîr before settling in a cave nearby at the edge of the "Everlasting" mountain—hewn with the tombs of the cult-goddess Hathor once worshiped in the pharaonic temples on the banks of the Nile at El-Qusiya. The cave became a second Bethlehem, and Coptic monks built a church there dedicated to the Virgin Mary. Even Muslim ladies went to it in hope of gaining favor.

Bishai Bey indeed had many reasons to believe in what the Lord had told Isaiah, "Blessed be Egypt my People." He owned four thousand *feddans* in the southern Nile Valley planted with cotton, wheat, maize, and barley. He also had succeeded his father as mayor of their tiny village. "He was the last mayor before the police took over," noted his great-grandson Magdi. "That was after he had built them a new station."

At age thirty, in 1920, Bishai was granted the Ottoman title of "bey" by the Sultan and future King Fuad. He also went on to win a senate seat in the first Egyptian parliament, standing for the Nationalist Party of Egypt's "savior," Saad Pasha Zaghloul. Yet all he had needed to do to beat out his political rival from neighboring El-Qusiya was to build a bigger and better house.

"It was a challenge to the family," his great-grandson recalled. "There was a lot of competition. The palace in El-Qusiya was similar to ours and also built by Italians." The fact that as an Orthodox Copt he did not "pray" did not seem to hurt Bishai's electoral chances against the Al-Azhar sheikh and governor of the province. Fortunately, Bishai had married his first cousin Salome, whose saintly ways smoothed over his sometimes difficult disposition. He also had built a church to the martyr saint Mercurius, known as Abu Seifein; the same saint's church in Old Cairo ranked as a museum of Coptic art.

A trip to see King Fuad in Alexandria brought Bishai Bey back home with Italian craftsmen and engineers for his new house. "It was like a *hôtel de ville*, with a pole outside flying a green flag with a crescent and three stars," his great-grandson recalled. Replacing the family's old stone fortress in the middle of fields, the residence became a palazzo—"with a reception house," the great-grandson insisted, referring to the *madyafa*, or "guest house," just inside the gate. As mayor, Bishai Bey oversaw village customs and served local justice in a plain room lined with wooden Ottoman divans. The salons on the upper floor, "more or less in the European style," according to Magdi, were to greet pilgrims traveling in the path of the Holy Family.

The Italian workmen added high towers at each corner of the new palazzo; its Tuscan floor plan called for terraces and balconies with balustrades that looked to the Nile on one side, and the Western Desert on the other. A central hallway led to a

OPPOSITE
With its high corner towers, the Italian villa seemed suited for one with the family name of Greiss, which in the ancient Coptic language means "small bell," presumably referring to a call to the faithful to seek a "blessing," or "grace."

To look closely at Bishai Bey's portrait is to see that his gallabiya was made of fine woven fabric.

OPPOSITE

A sacred aura emanates from the central hall and side rooms of a villa built in a countryside that has witnessed the rule of pharaohs, holds traditions about the footsteps of the Holy Family, and was settled by early Christian Greeks whose literary rolls of papyrus in the royal necropolis at Mîr included works by Aristotle.

marble staircase, which rose to the family's private quarters above; there, a large stair hall gave onto several apartments, one for Bishai's only child, Wahiba, and her husband. "She was 'the Lady of the Castle,' and very strong," noted her grandson. "He had spoiled her."

The Italians indulged their rococo tastes for finely carved and finished woodwork and exquisitely plastered and painted walls in the main reception salons. "Few believed that this could exist outside of Cairo," declared Magdi. A formal sitting room offered visitors what in Upper Egypt was a surprising combination of pastel pink and green lacquered walls with matching fabrics for upholstered canapés and side chairs. A dining room with a coffered ceiling "was a smaller version of Abdin palace," he further noted. "We also had a 'dumb-waiter,' an elevator, coming up from the kitchen in the basement."

"My great-grandfather was one of the last to have slaves," Magdi also revealed. Of the thirteen, some nine worked as house servants, helping host as many as one hundred guests during election campaigns. Two Sudanese cooks, "like Cordon Bleu chefs," worked off big charcoal ranges, serving Egyptian and continental dishes. "My great-grandfather liked grilled pigeons flambéed in imported cognac—Rémy Martin," added Magdi, noting that Bishai had built many houses out back for the birds. Otherwise, there was "St. George rum" to sip on. "It was cold there at night."

Imitating an Old-World European look in 1924 did not mean Bishai was to skimp on modern conveniences. An Italian mechanic living in Mîr installed a generator for electricity, and a boiler in the basement provided heat to the house, which eventually had its own power station. Yet that was not to be the only "miracle." The lacquered walls would remain as fresh as new over the years, leaving everyone to wonder if they too had been "blessed."

The paint on the walls and ceiling, which is more than eighty years old, looks as fresh as if it had been applied yesterday here in the dry desert climate of Upper Egypt.

A coffered ceiling, carved pediment surrounds over doorways, and parquet floors recall the great dining hall of Abdin Palace—suggesting that the same Italian artisans who had worked for Egypt's rulers also were here, or at least craftsmen who had trained under them.

VILLA OF THE PAPAL NUNCIO

Zamalek, Cairo. 1927

T he old Franciscan could hardly believe his eyes. The bougainvilleas he had planted by the river had exploded into a blaze of fuchsia overnight. It was a good omen for Pius XI and his new villa in Cairo. Disembarking from his boat, Monsignor Andrea Cassulo made his way toward the broad, front steps with an agility that belied his age. The outgoing apostolic delegate did not expect posterity to remember his name, but he knew the villa he was about to bless would not be forgotten—even long after the once-marshy north side of Gezira island had grown into the fashionable Cairo residential district of Zamalek.

Monsignor Cassulo had not had to look far to find an Italian architect worthy of the commission. Domenico Limongelli was already established with his older brother, Alessandro, in the family construction firm in Alexandria. Managing local projects for architects back in Italy, he had become well-versed in a variety of historical styles. He had also learned an important lesson for building in Egypt: the best-laid plans counted little unless the caprices of sand or a muddy river shoreline were conquered. By 1914 Limongelli's technical bureau in Cairo was doing a brisk business specializing in "Fondations de toute nature."

Limongelli's career received an enormous boost from his marriage to the daughter of Artin Pasha, a government minister of Armenian origin who was also a noted conservationist and director of the prestigious Institute of Egypt. The forty-seven-year-old architect had burst onto the Cairo social scene, and began to leap rapidly from one commission to another. Italians were especially loved by King Fuad, who had lived and studied in Italy, and Limongelli went from riverside villas in the exclusive district of Giza to a new Coptic church in suburban Matariya dedicated to the Virgin Mary to Latin churches and religious institutes. His work for the pope, who exhibited amazing prescience when he transferred his envoy's residence to Cairo from Alexandria, was perhaps his most heartfelt.

The pope's new villa was modeled on the early houses of the Medicis in the countryside outside Florence—handsome, fortified havens for a family that had yet to establish its dynastic power and develop a taste for luxury. Pulling plans out of the architecture books to create an eye-catching sight on the shore did not mean Limongelli held back on satisfying his own instincts. Why not an open-air top floor with a terrace under the exposed wooden rafters of a red clay tiled roof? Surely the papal nuncio would appreciate the cool river breezes and distant views in every direction! It was an idea that would have made the imperial Romans smile, Monsignor Cassulo reflected proudly, watching solemnly as the papal keys rose up along the Nile for the first time.

Limongelli's villa was large for the piece of land it stood on, but later destiny brought in some breathing room: adjoining lots split off from the domain of the religious sisters of the Central African Mission. They had received a big chunk of the then-unwanted northern end of the island after fleeing the Sudan in the 1880s. Limongelli also prevailed in silencing critics from the

The office and residence of the papal nuncio hugs the banks of the Nile on the island of Gezira and its once exclusive suburb of Zamalek, where the Comboni missionaries of central Africa were granted terrains by a munificent Khedive Tewfik.

161

Did architect Domenico Limongelli intend to give the pope in Rome a villa with an open roof terrace to enjoy the prevailing summer breeze from the north? Or was he thinking of the early Medici family in Tuscany, and a lookout for any sign of trouble on the Nile?

OPPOSITE

The central hall of the papacy's villa was a perfect solution to its need for a side staircase to the private quarters above, a dining room, a chapel, a small parlor, a great reception space, and offices for the representatives of Pius XI, who had made a personal decision to establish a presence of the Holy See in Cairo.

past who had dismissed the Holy See's churches, schools, convents, monasteries, institutes, hospices, and charities as having little or no architectural merit. Here in a villa that resonated with the hillsides of Tuscany were not only elegant arcaded terraces, balustrade balconies, and generous windows, but a plan not seen elsewhere in Cairo. A number of rooms emanated from a long central hall: a grand salon, a chapel, a dining room, the envoy's office, and tucked away at the far end, an elegant marble staircase. Limongelli had sensed the papacy's future: two short years later Pius XI had gained an independent Vatican City, Italy had adopted Roman Catholicism as its state religion, and Egypt had become a nation.

ROYAL LEGATION OF ITALY

Garden City, Cairo. 1927–30

W orking in his studio in Rome, the architect Florestano Di Fausto leaned back from his drawing board and took a long moment to think. Just returned from four years of building and rebuilding on the island of Rhodes, he had learned to adapt to all sorts of circumstances. Now, in 1927, at age thirty-seven, he felt seriously challenged. He had to design diplomatic quarters worthy of the Italian government in Cairo.

The site in the exclusive enclave of Garden City was exceptional, for it overlooked the Nile. Yet it also was hemmed in by side streets, one branching off at an abrupt angle from the road along the riverbank. What could Di Fausto do with this long, narrow, and oddly triangular islet? Il Duce was in power; national pride was at stake. Di Fausto's own humble beginnings only prodded him further to give his best.

Di Fausto's thoughts turned to the Nile. Why not design a building as if it were a sailing vessel pulled in alongside the water's edge? Disregarding the fact that his building would only clear the road beside the river by inches, Di Fausto drew a façade to be viewed from the perspective of the water. In walls of red brick and rubble stone, he envisioned seven windows with pediments in the style of Michelangelo and a massive, rusticated entrance with granite Ionic columns. Di Fausto might have enjoyed playing with the contrasts and juxtapositions of modernism, adding unframed and irregularly placed windows, or square and circular openings near the roof line. But he remained loyal to historical tradition, as he would his entire career; nor did he need reminding that Egypt had once been a possession of imperial Rome.

Three wide arches marked the passage from the residence to the chancery façade, and here Di Fausto conjured up one of the building's most curious attractions. Set into an oblong gray stone plaque was a great sundial inscribed "An observation of the hour of the winter solstice." The moment in late December when the sun shifts in its path and starts again to move northward had been celebrated since antiquity as a rebirth, a time of perfect harmony. Was Di Fausto thinking of the Italian Renaissance, and Dante's frenzied vision of early dawn, and the first trembling rays of light across a distant ocean? Perhaps the architect was remembering his experience on Rhodes, the new Italian possession off Asia Minor that had once been the domain of Helios, the Greek god of the sun also worshiped in ancient Egypt. To a graduate of the Academy of Fine Arts in Rome, such symbols were profoundly resonant.

With the building's "stern," and its bow window, facing south to overlook a small enclosed garden, anyone rounding the bend in the river road to the north suddenly squared-up face-to-face with the ship-of-state and its "prow" at the tip of an islet. There, midway up, was a carved stone medallion of Caesar flanked by muscular Roman men in the Fascist style of the day.

Di Fausto left the actual construction of his building to his able compatriot Paolo Caccia Dominioni, who would later design the Italian war memorial at El-Alamein. Contracting with the Di Farro construction firm, long favored by the Egyptian

OPPOSITE
Selecting a side wall to be
seen from both the street
and the Nile, architect Di
Fausto designed a plaque
with a sundial marking the
winter solstice — an event
tied to ancient traditions and
the Italian Renaissance and
ideas of rebirth. Was Di
Fausto also paying homage
to the ancient Egyptians,
who believed in resurrection
and future life?

OVERLEAF
Both the decorator
Melchiorre Bega from
Bologna and Di Fausto had
previously worked with the
marble suppliers to the
Vatican, the firm of Paolo
Medici & Figlio. The firm
shipped the white and gray-
veined and pink marble for
the staircase, as well as
for a variety of fireplaces
in the building.

ABOVE LEFT
Architect Florentano Di
Fausto adapted well to
varying circumstances, and
the same pediment windows
he used in Cairo would also
appear in his work in Tunis
and in Nice. But did he
imagine his bow window
facing south would give such
a perfect impression of the
stern of a sailing vessel
along the Nile?

ABOVE RIGHT
Collaborating with Di Fausto
on a number of projects,
among them the royal opera
house of Rome, the
decorator Melchiorre Bega
worked here with local
counterpart Enrico Nistri,
originally from Pisa; the
Milanese-born engineer and
architect Paolo Caccia
Dominioni had executed Di
Fausto's building plans.

royal court, Paolo also oversaw the interior decoration by Melchiorre Bega. The architect from Bologna—whose family went on to become Italy's best-known decorators and furniture manufacturers—fit Di Fausto like a hand in a glove, despite their very different temperaments. Bega carried on Di Fausto's themes as if they had been his own. Not even thirty, he was as much a showman as Di Fausto, and was fast to impress with his clean, bold lines of Art Deco.

Bega's lavish use of mirrors, Ionic columns, and the finest marbles to be seen outside Italy announced his intentions clearly as soon as one stepped through the front doorway. A hard-edged double staircase in the small entrance vestibule had been expertly crafted in white-veined marble by the renowned Vatican suppliers Paolo Medici & Figlio. Five fireplaces in stones ranging from *verde antico* and porphyry to pearl-white and black onyx also offered a rare sight in Cairo.

Bega also devised spacious reception areas with pairs of columns on stands of yet more green marble. Repeating geometric patterns divided up the vast ceiling of the main hall, whose far wall was devoted to the bow window. Preoccupied with light and space, Bega added squares of mirrors to five sets of double doors, and installed tall lampposts of Murano crystal and chandeliers with wrought-iron arms and branches.

As the decorator of the Genoese cruise ship *Conte di Savoia*, Bega was the most sought-after designer of naval interiors. It was no surprise then that he carried over many ideas from his naval work into a dining room paneled in fine woods with matching table and chairs. To his partner's approval, Bega recognized that this was no ordinary waterside palazzo, but the finest luxury ship ever to sail the Nile.

EL-CHENNAOUI HOUSE

Mansoura, province of Dakahliya. 1928

I t took the marriage of Mohamed Bey Mohamed's second of two sons to bring out the "Voice of Egypt." But there she was, Oum Kalhsoum, the "Daughter of the Delta," performing at her poetic best in the Chennaouis' back garden. With her head tilted back, her eyelids lowered, and arms raised high, a long transparent foulard falling from her fingertips, she had grown men weeping that night. No longer the small Bedouin girl dressed as a boy and chanting liturgical verses to the fellaheen picking cotton, she had yet to appear in Chanel and dark glasses or give gala performances at the Olympia in Paris. But she surely was *El-Sett*, "The Lady."

And she was great. "We built a tent for the guests," the bridegroom, Saad, recalled years later, noting that it had extended from the house past the tennis court and fountains to the rose bushes and mango trees by the river. "Nokrashi Pasha came," he went on to say with pride, adding that the future prime minister had been among the gentlemen who heard "The Cotton Is Open," "The Flowers Are Beautiful," "All Good Friends," even "My Love is Waiting." As for the ladies, "The music reached us through the microphones," reported the youngest of Saad's six sisters. The ladies were listening upstairs in the French salon where they met to tell their secrets and arrange weddings and engagements. "My mother had chosen my wife," Saad also remembered.

Why had Mohamed Bey built a villa on the Damietta branch of the Nile that seemed to belong to southern Italy? Descending from a family of merchants who took farmland as payment for outstanding bills, "it was known he owned half of Mansoura, nearly," Saad recounted. Mohamed also had furthered his father's industries in cotton, rice, sugar, carpentry, and ironworks. In the 1920s, according to his son, he had erected "high buildings and a palace" with Italian workers. Construction still was the domain of the Italians, who had made Mansoura a center for home furnishings. "Some Italian engineers had seen a postcard of the palace of the King of Italy and made a copy of it for our house," Saad revealed.

No doubt they had tried to produce their best for a family that not only had survived Napoleon's invasion but traced their lineage back to the Crusades and a captive "sultan of France." The Italians produced exuberant carved plasterwork, wooden paneling, and intricate ironworks to rival the palaces of the Khedive Ismail himself. In fact they would win for Mohamed Bey a gold medal for architecture at the Fiera Esposizione Al Litorrale in Bologna in 1931. A framed certificate hung on a wall in a reception salon next to a picture of Mussolini.

"Since my grandfather's time the Chennaoui house had been an open one, especially during Ramadan," Saad went on. The villa became known as the local Beit el-Oumma, the "House of the Nation." A columned porch out front with wicker tables and side chairs surely was a welcoming sign of hospitality. And a Pierce Arrow with silver-plated fittings "even had the pashas coming to look at it," Saad noted. "It was known father had political ambitions. He liked to invite everyone, from a royal prince

The Italian artisans added stucco garlands, panels and crowns, crystal wall sconces, and other decorative accessories to a central hall dominated by a great ebony staircase that had been sent from Italy in one entire piece.

The Italians had produced
everything they could think
of in terms of decorative
stuccowork for the
Chennaoui villa's façade:
including, at the top, and at
center, a rococo shield for a
coat-of-arms that looked
like those in the West.

to the poor people," Saad recalled. "We had a salon in the basement that was open every night all year long. It had a billiards table and a shoe-shine, and closed at midnight." Sometimes there were social miscalculations, however. "Everybody had heard about the wedding," Saad went on. "They thought it was an open house, but they did not let people in and they revolted."

"My mother had a day each week to see her friends," Saad also reported. And to look at the high crown moldings and silk brocade walls and suites of gilt Louis XVI armchairs, the furniture-makers of Mansoura were adept at supplying the local taste for bourgeois comfort. With his brother's move to Cairo, Saad was left behind to reside in the dim baroque salons with exquisite parquet floors crafted by locals taught by Italian *moallems*, or masters.

Any lack of luxury on the main floor compared with the salons for the ladies above was offset at least in part by a handsome solid-ebony staircase. Rising up at one side of the central hall, the staircase had been sent in one piece from Italy. Mohamed Bey himself had brought back from Italy a collection of figures in copper, which he displayed in his own rooms overlooking the back gardens. The same Italians working on King Fuad's palace at Montaza evidently had extra floral floor tiles to spare for use also on Mohamed Bey's columned balcony.

"If the Chennaoui house was known for anything, it was famous for its feasts," Saad declared. "We used to have more than twenty people working at home full-time," he said. To have three cooks in a basement kitchen meant combining traditional Egyptian food with Turkish in a way that made them nearly inseparable. The food was sent up by "an elevator" to a wooden-paneled dining hall and served on Haviland porcelain from Limoges. At the center of each piece, including the tea cups for the ladies, were the initials MC, denoting the Frenchified name of its owner Mohamed Chennaoui.

But while the Chennaouis might have felt Europeanized, their guest Oum Kalhsoum remained true to her provincial nature. "Thanks again to you all, people of Mansoura, natives of the Delta. I never forget that my force always comes from here."

The rosewood paneling of this study, like teak, sandalwood, jujubier, ebony, and other fine woods, was considered the height of luxurious decoration in a country like Egypt.

Where else could the Italians best show off their talents than in the city that had become the decorations capital of Egypt once the Khedive Ismail had built his palaces here along the Nile? They would give the Chennaoui villa a carnival of decorative details for ceilings and walls also inlaid with silk-lined panels.

BADRAWI-ASHUR PALACE

Drîn, province of Dakahliya. 1930s

Sayed Pasha was no magician. But he could turn Delta mud into gold, and make a palace that looked like Abdin and its five hundred rooms appear out of nowhere in the middle of the countryside. He always insisted that he was a simple peasant, rising at dawn each day, downing his vegetables and *'aish baladi*—local bread—before heading out into the muddy fields in his white gallabiya. Except that trailing behind him in the latest-model tractors and trucks were his seven sons, assorted nephews, and grandsons, also clad in white, to be spotted from afar as bona fide Badrawis in their lands as big as a small state.

Sayed Pasha had gone into big-time modern farming, mechanized irrigation, and airplanes for spraying crops long before the giant corporations arrived to conquer world agriculture. Everyone knew the Badrawi name from office buildings and apartment houses in Cairo. But as head of the family Sayed Pasha was not amused by the full-page spreads in the popular *El-Massawar* magazine in 1933 proclaiming the Badrawis "the Rockefellers of Egypt." For him the other family members could keep their urban buildings, which only meant that "the porters go off with your money when you sleep at night." He had taken as gospel truth an Al-Azhar sheikh's opinion forbidding the earning of interest and stuck to the best way he knew for reinvesting: harvests. Send profits abroad? "Why do that? We come from the mud of Egypt!"

And what mud! Having some 36,000 *feddans* planted mostly with cotton yielding three crops a year often meant each Badrawi logged in fifty miles a day as they trekked through sandy roads as far north as the Mediterranean—only getting back to Drîn after six at night, or to a twin palace in the nearby village of Bhut belonging to Sayed's brother Mohamed. Another good way to reinvest! The two palaces had been built by Italians after the family's old wooden *harmalik* at Drîn had burnt down, leaving only a *salamlik*, or reception house. When Sayed Pasha was around the lights went out early. "He's coming, he's coming," the youngsters at Drîn relayed back from the high stone gates out front, sounding the alarm through the long halls to stop the music, the poker games, and whatever else had needed closed doors in front of the approaching pasha. *Yalla, Basha.*

Everybody knew that hard work had made the Badrawis the farm kings of Egypt and one of its richest families. So great was their success at reclaiming salty lands to the west of the Nile branch ending at Damietta that many wondered if the Badrawis were planning to take over the Mediterranean! They had started in the mid-nineteenth century when a peasant in the small village of Bhut called Badrawi Ashur had picked up on the Khedive Ismail's offering of free lands and easy taxes to those able to make them farmable. Badrawi Ashur succeeded, going on to become *'omda*, or mayor, of Bhut, and even bought some "good land" on installment.

Sayed was no Turkish pasha lording it over his peasants. "He was a peasant himself," his grandson Raouf recalled. "A rich one, yes, but a peasant." Arriving from Cairo, it was off with the coats and ties, and out of sight with the black Rolls Royce. "We were not exactly going out to ride horses," Raouf went on. "Everyone had his own mission. And everything was well-run."

Who would have expected a residence in the eastern Delta resembling the Abdin Palace, home of the Egyptian rulers in Cairo?

OPPOSITE
The main entrance hall and its marble staircase, which leads to the same plan above, is the central point from which extend the long wings of the Badrawi-Ashur Palace.

ABOVE
Columns along the wide corridor of a wing of the Badrawi-Ashur Palace help demarcate public sitting areas and salons, while to the sides are sleeping chambers and other rooms.

It was one big estate; our shares were in *sheyoui*, or common ground." And there was no letting up on Sayed's etiquette in treating his own family the same way as his workers. "Don't think you're any better than any of them!" he was to scold a son standing under the shade of a sycamore tree, leaving the fellaheen out in the fierce hot sun.

What better way to keep his sons down on the farm than in a palace? "Drîn was made up of four big wings," Raouf remembered. "We each took a wing, the first four of us, the rest going into side apartments," he went on. "We only really had three or four rooms for ourselves when everyone thought we were living in a huge palace."

The Drîn and Bhut palaces were marvels of Italian building. The amount of Carrara marble that went for staircases, halls, columns, and vast floor spaces could only be expressed in terms of tonnage. The front steps at Bhut were best described as the width of a good-sized tractor four times over! At Drîn each of the side wings on two floors was decorated differently. "We each had a theme," Raouf went on. "One was black lacquer with gold. . . . Ours was French." The long wing became a reception hall, filled with Aubusson carpets, French and Italian paintings, furniture from Maison Kriéger, the Paris decorations house. The other rooms "were more cozy, each like a small salon." The family did not need summer trips to Europe, and especially Paris, to decorate. "There was nothing really new for us to buy. We had everything here." Even King Farouk, who came to Drîn in 1948 for the opening of a hospital built by the family, was impressed enough to remark: "I now know why you stay in the countryside."

ABAZA VILLA

Robamiya, province of Sharkiya. 1932

I n the late eighteenth century, a tribe of Bedouins originally from Yemen had barely moved from tents to houses in the eastern Delta when one of its sheikhs made a very unconventional move: He married a lady from outside his tribe! A Circassian, she was as beautiful as any favorite of the Ottoman Sultan, the Shah of Persia, or the Khedive of Egypt. Her dignity and grace were such that one of her grandsons adopted as his family name that of her native home, Abkhazia, in the western Caucasus. His family in Egypt thus came to be known as Abaza.

"The Circassian lady also must have been rich and powerful because her husband took her to a place away from the rest of the tribe and built her a new house," noted one of her descendants, Mahmoud Abaza.

The Abazas thereafter went on to have many more residences, including, in 1932, their "New House." By that time the family in Egypt was heading toward numbering twelve thousand or more, with many branches and wide connections. At various times they would own and control nearly the entire province of Sharkiya east of the Nile—a remarkable feat for the tribe of Al-Aidh Bedouins, who had crossed the Suez desert in the thirteenth century. Even the Egyptian encyclopedist Ali Pasha Mubarak had noted in 1887 that these "coarse nomads" had been "lucky before and after the arrival of Islam."

"We're still a tribe more than a family!" declared Mahmoud. And perhaps the luck is still also there. The Abaza name appears across the country on tractor-trailer vehicles, as the name of tea salons and coffee shops, and even as a name used by people who are not part of the family.

The family had remained regional. "Very few of us left our rural homes, except to go to school in Cairo," explained Mahmoud. But the Abazas were hardly country farmers. The family boasted ten pashas and a running total of six members of parliament, according to Mahmoud, "except in 1950, when we had eight." One, uncle Aziz Pasha, was not only a formidable civil servant, but a romantic epic poet of some renown. The oldest son of Mohamed Pasha, he "died fighting the war against free verse," offered Mahmoud. Like all Abazas, he always returned to Sharqiya for the holidays. Mahmoud's father had stayed at home on the land and found the architect for the house.

At twenty-five, Aziz's younger brother Ahmed had discovered the talents of a classmate of his cousin's at the École Polytechnique in Cairo. He was Mustapha Pasha Fahmy, and a year after awarding its first diploma in architecture in 1933, the school had granted him a teaching chair and the title of *ustaz*, or professor—making him one of the first two Egyptians to join the faculty of this largely foreign-run institution. Ahmed asked Fahmy to design a classical house with "modern materials," by which he meant something other than traditional Turkish wooden construction. "Stone also was inexpensive," Mahmoud noted.

Mustapha Pasha Fahmy surely seemed to be thinking of pharaohs when he designed this entrance gate for a family long established in the province of Sharkiya and having its branch of Abazas settled in an area that once was a domain of *robamiya*, or "four hundred," *feddans.*

177

Evidently having sketched some plans for the Abazas in Robamiya, it seemed as if architect Mustapha Pasha Fahmy was paying tribute to the vertical line of date palms and other tall arbors nearby, as well as to the pharaohs, when he added bold and unadorned portal columns to their "New House."

Aziz Abaza's wife, Emina Sidky, had added mirrors to built-in shelves to help brighten an interior sitting room.

OPPOSITE

No wonder the portrait of Hasan Pasha appears at top and center of a gallery alcove in a sitting room of the Abazas' country house: a contemporary of the ruler Mohamed Ali Pasha, he was the one to establish the Abaza name in Egypt.

An Abaza cousin executed Fahmy's plans for a simple stone house fronted by columns. Ancient Egyptian motifs were nothing new to Fahmy, who was inspired by the Old Kingdom site of Tell Basta nearby. Three years earlier he also had built a temple-like mausoleum in Cairo for the Nationalist Party leader Saad Pasha Zaghloul.

"We called it the 'New House' because it replaced our old stone house and its annexes," Mahmoud went on, referring to a residential complex built by his grandfather Mohamed Pasha, one of twelve sons and seven daughters of Osman Abaza, a one-time civil servant at Abdin palace. It had been 1840 when Osman first built a family house on lands that he had inherited west of the provincial capital of Zagazig and south of the Bahr Moïs, or Meweiss Canal, once the ancient Tanic arm of the Nile.

Mohamed Pasha needed "a big house" to accommodate his retinue of ladies. Married three times after first taking a bride in 1879, he built a stone house with an octagonal hall that would retain warmth in the winter and dissipate heat in summer. The hall was the main salon, "with two Napoleon III sofas, four fauteuils, and twelve chairs," Mahmoud noted, adding "my father later put in a bathroom, and a second floor kitchenette." After Mohamed Pasha died in 1931, "it was impossible to keep the old aunts in a house that was falling down and had forty-six people living in it."

The "New House" stood at the end of a long, leafy drive. A broad terrace on one side overlooked open fields beyond a grove of banyan trees—the giant aerial roots appearing like a piece of modern sculpture. "We still had a *salamlik*," noted Mahmoud, "a *madyafa*, or office, a salon *shetoui* for the winter's sun, and a salon *bahri* facing north in summer." A spacious central hall gave off to good-sized salons for political meetings, tea-time gatherings, reading, or plain relaxing. "As each son got married, a wing was added," further noted Mahmoud.

The greatest changes to the "New House" arrived when Aziz Pasha remarried after his wife's death. His new wife was Emina, the daughter of one-time prime minister Ismail Sidqi, and former wife of a member of the Egyptian royal family. "She was a painter," Mahmoud recalled. "I wouldn't say how good of a painter, but she had studied at the Beaux-Arts in Paris." Emina changed beige walls to orange, white, blue, and even green, and took out windows to put up mirrors in order to brighten the central hall. She also introduced tapestries, and brought in Art Deco chairs from France, crystal chandeliers, and other furnishings found in "stores in Cairo which then were *très à la mode*," said Mahmoud. "All the newly married ladies took Emina's advice," he added. As it turned out, "she would have the biggest influence on all the Abaza houses for the next thirty years."

SPAHI HOUSE

Alexandria. 1926–30 and thereafter

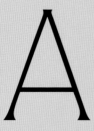

Abdul-Hamid's two older brothers thought his idea of buying a villa at the beginning of a war was little short of crazy. Yet the upstart Syrian businessman from Aleppo was determined. Not yet thirty, he could think of nothing better than to live behind high stone walls in the exclusive Alexandria suburb of Ramleh. He had several growing children, with more on the way, and they needed outdoor space for play. Besides, Ramleh was the "Egyptian Riviera," with a long and beautiful sandy coastline.

Abdul-Hamid's timing was perfect. A Lebanese family had put its large residence up for sale, and the architect Ferdinand Debanne agreed to freshen up the classic Art Deco villa to suit its new owners. The debonair Debanne, with his three-piece suit and pipe, gave the house designed by Georges Parq and Max Edrei a dash of youthful chic, as he adapted it for a life of entertaining, both indoors and out.

Abdul-Hamid had already known Debanne—his ancestors were Lebanese-Syrians—and had commissioned him before the war to design a new textile factory southeast of town. The architect's long, low building, with its high clock-tower became the factory that would make the Spahi logo famous. It was soon the largest privately owned factory in the country, just behind the two state-owned giants. After the war, Abdul-Hamid had more than ten thousand workers turning out yarn and finished goods for export, and would see his dream come true when he replaced his second-hand machines with new ones bought in China.

New machines were not enough to amuse Abdul-Hamid's young wife, however. The lovely, dark-haired Fadila was more concerned that her house needed furnishing. Although she had inherited her Syrian mother's good taste along with her grand town house in Aleppo, it was by the sea at Izmir that she had felt most at home. On the eve of their move to Alexandria in 1938 at twenty-two, the first thing Fadila would ask her husband was, "Do they have a sea over there?" and he was glad to reassure her, "They certainly do!"

The wind-battered Mediterranean coast was not the Aegean. Yet one still could ride a donkey over to the beach, or take the "corniche" road out to the Aleppo pines at Montaza, or even jump on one of the electric trams that ran back and forth into town through the dunes. New bathing cabins soon arrived at the sandy crescent of Stanley Bay nearby, and the waterside Casino Chatby had a swank restaurant and dancing to a jazz orchestra at night. For a sophisticated private occasion, however, nothing could match the Spahi House.

Debanne brought in suites of sleekly upholstered sofas and side chairs covered in French blue silk, which worked nicely in a central hall broken up by tall square columns. Guests were made to feel just as comfortable in the more intimate adjoining salons, with Louis XVI canapés, wooden parquet, and carpets. "They had Turkish divans in Izmir, but my parents only brought the carpets with them, very old ones, not like the copies in Alexandria," reported Fadila's daughter Emira, speaking in French.

Entertaining at the Spahi House often spilled over into a garden of pebble-stone pathways, a pergola, and two rectangular fish "ponds"; one, inside a trellised kiosk, was tiled in sea-green ceramics and decorated at night with colored lights.

LEFT
Who could not have wanted to dine, dance, or listen to music in Ferdinand Debanne's cabaret room? The architect and decorator had filled the Spahi House's entire ground level with Art Deco sofas and side chairs framed in a checkerboard of various woods.

RIGHT
Ferdinand Debanne also brought his Art Deco style to the Spahi House's red lacquered ground-floor walls and, for a small alcove for parlor games, the same red with a repeating pattern of dancers.

She still spoke Arabic with her mother's Syrian accent, but noted that her Turkish was still good, although now she "only heard it on television."

A dining room paneled in light oak at the far end of the reception hall offered something unique for Egyptians—a fireplace. Facing west, the room overlooked a terrace, and beyond, tidy beds of flowers, stone pathways, a pergola, and two rectangular fish ponds. Besides a staff of four maids, two gardeners, two chauffeurs, and a security guard, there were a full-time chef and assistant to oversee the huge white kitchen. This included a separate pantry, almost as big as the kitchen itself, which accommodated a refrigerator with a freezer shipped from Izmir. According to Emira, "Ice had not yet come to Alexandria."

Debanne attended carefully to every detail of the food service. Delivery out back was to be as easy as the meal's arrival by dumb-waiter in the dining room a floor higher. Across from the kitchen was a second dining area that seated thirty, with smoky gray mirrors magnifying the space.

On the ground floor, Debanne lacquered the walls in fire-engine red and black, and added frescoes of fanciful ballerinas and small repeating Art Deco patterns to create an area for parlor games. Three-piece suites of contemporary furniture broke up the open floor space, and a black upright piano came to life at the regular New Year's masked ball. The gentlemen came in "white tie and *smoking*, the ladies in *robes de soirée*," Emira recalled, "the latest fashions from Paris," from the Cairo branches of Hannaux and Chalon.

Debanne broke away from his favored Art Deco in Fadila's bedroom, where lengths of pale blue silk and tulle covering beds and windows recalled eighteenth-century France. The fabrics did not come from Spahi mills, however. Like all the fabrics in the house, they were imported.

A sitting room of the Spahi
House that once was its
dining room still features an
Art Deco chandelier with
Greek key fretwork, and a
fireplace and hood of carved
teak and decorated with a
band of lotus flowers.

OPPOSITE
Ferdinand Debanne added apple-
green painted walls and a vivid
portrait of Fadila to the main
parlor filled with a suite of
French furniture—preferred by
Alexandrians "over the British
or German styles because of its
light wood," notes a descendant
of the city's premier dealer in
antique furniture, Habashi.

HAMED SAID STUDIO AND HOUSE

El-Marg. 1942–45

Hamed Said and his wife were both artists. They had been working together in a secluded spot in the Muqattam hills just above Cairo's ancient citadel when a new highway abruptly did away with their studio, and their precious sense of tranquility. They set out in search of a new place that would offer them the same peace of mind and spirit of their lost abode, and soon settled on a tract of land near El-Marg, an *ezbet*, or tiny settlement, north of the city. The atmosphere came close to a romantic Corot landscape, but with green open fields giving way instead to date-palms and papyrus marshes edging the desert.

Hamed and his wife, Ehsan Khalil, at first stayed in a tent on their land to get a feeling for the place. They were filled with light, and they could breathe. "When we came here, we had only green agricultural fields and the desert. . . . That is why we came. We came to understand how agriculture can give birth to civilization and art," recalled Hamed, well into his nineties. A botanical watercolorist schooled in London, he paused briefly. "We discovered that in the plant you can find the secret and the logic of life, the meaning of truth and justice, which in Egypt we call *Maat*." The concept dates back to the pharaohs, who personified Maat as a goddess symbolized by an ostrich feather. "We wanted to live here to understand our discovery more deeply."

The couple initially had wished for a studio away from their apartment in Cairo. They then decided to spend weekends camping on their land to plan for a house. "It is a well-known fact that agriculture and culture are twins," interjected Hamed, who taught science until 1936. The two artists invited the architect Hassan Fathy to stay with them, putting up another tent so that he too could get a feeling for the place. "He was my friend," declared Hamed with a reflective, far-reaching look. "We were made to be close friends, complete friends. We had no disagreements. On the contrary, we had the same ideas."

Fathy had been commissioned a year earlier by the Royal Society of Agriculture to build a granary. Since the cost of importing wood from war-torn Europe was prohibitive, he had gone to Aswan to study traditional Nubian methods of building. There he found in mud brick an alternative to wood and industrial concrete—a material which, in any case, he loathed. "He was like many original thinkers who do not invent, but rather discover," reasoned Hamed.

The couple was inspired by the simple spaces of the vaults and domes of his granary, and asked Fathy to design a similar building for their home. They joined him in creating its intimate and refined spaces, and even years later, the special aura of the house would continue to impress visitors. The house—the first signed by Fathy using the mud-brick technique—would serve as a prototype for his village of New Gourna near Luxor. Although that project was never realized, it paved the way for his Architecture for the Poor.

Fathy began with a simple, harmonious plan for his friends at El-Marg: an enclosed, domed space for a studio; an adjoining *iwan*, or alcove, for sleeping; and a vaulted loggia where the couple could sit and enjoy the green paradise around

Hassan Fathy's signature dome rises up from his mud-brick house for his friends Hamed Said and his wife, while wicker armchairs, according to Egyptian taste, line the walls along the entryway as if they were the divans of past times.

PREVIOUS LEFT
A pharaonic bust in a recess
of the corridor leading to
the artists' studio gives the
feeling that this was a
transit to a sacred area.

PREVIOUS RIGHT
With a need to unite
two areas of his friends'
residence, Hassan Fathy
created drama by adding a
series of recesses and insets
of windows to one side to
give place for Hamed Said
to display his replicas of
pharaonic busts.

ABOVE
The entry door is carved
with the Coptic cross for
Ehsan Khalil, who is
a Christian.

OPPOSITE
Hassan Fathy designed not
only the studio and house,
but the furniture as well.
Shown here on the right are
two versions of Mahmoud
Mukhtar's sculpture, "The
Eternal Egyptian Woman."

them. Hamed and Ehsan were so delighted by the arrangement that three years later they asked Fathy to add an extension so they could live there as well. For this second phase, completed in 1945, the architect worked around several date-palm trees that the couple had planted in order "to know life." To accommodate the trees, Fathy designed a central inner courtyard, which later became the meeting place for a group known as The Friends of Art and Life. Headed by Hamed, it included, among others, artists, architects—including Fathy—sculptors, weavers, and potters.

Forming part of the house's U-shaped central enclosure was a wing for a kitchen, a dining room, and a bathroom. A gallery with a skylight ran the length of the original first section and linked up harmoniously with another new addition that included a large vaulted studio. "He made those vaults for a certain use, for creating sculpture," noted Ehsan, a textile-designer, adding, "Hamed stood under every curve," every one of them, going from one into another and in every direction. "Yes," confirmed Hamed, "I was following them all . . . knowing that the proportion in every curve, in its essence, was like a touch in a drawing."

The gallery ended with a corner for meditation with views of the inner courtyard that created an almost sacred spatial effect. At Hamed's request, a line of recesses with lancet windows was added to display his collection of pharaonic busts. He spoke of the gallery wistfully. For many years the couple had lived without the desire or need for electricity. On some nights a single flickering candle brought dramatic movement to the stillness and shadows, illuminating what meant most to this extraordinary couple, a magical interlude of art and life.

TOUSSOUN ABU GABAL HOUSE

Giza. 1947

T he Second World War was pressing on, and Toussoun Abu Gabal needed to move fast. At twenty-three, he had stayed behind in Paris long enough to finish his degree in agricultural sciences. Now it was time to go. Luckily, he had the company of his brother-in-law for the long drive home by way of Istanbul. A diplomat of Iraqi descent and his senior by many years, Taher Bey El-Omari was Egypt's departing consul general to France. He also was a connoisseur of literature, fine arts, and music. One of his close friends in Paris had shared his passion for classical music, and Taher would later introduce him to Toussoun. He was the architect Hassan Fathy.

Taher was among Fathy's first clients in Egypt in the late 1930s. The war had cut off building supplies from Europe and prices had skyrocketed. Fathy thus set aside his classical training for a vision of traditional and affordable Egyptian mud brick. Yet his domed house for Taher in the Faiyoum never got beyond the drawing board, for, as a cousin, Mohamed Shawki explained, "Uncle Taher was very formal and highly cultivated. But . . . he was very—how do you say?—*bourgeois guindé*, Straight as an arrow." And Fathy? "He was an artist, living for his ideas and ideals."

By the end of the war, with plenty of cash coming in from the agricultural land he had inherited in Middle Egypt, the young Toussoun decided to invest in Cairo real estate. One lot in Giza just behind the Nileside residence of the Turkish ambassador struck him as perfect for a town house for himself and his new wife. It also suited his plans for an apartment building to rent out to Taher and his sisters. "Toussoun was very rich, but careful with his money. And I mean very careful!" reported Mohamed Shawki. "The house was really for Taher."

Toussoun nonetheless had also warmed to Fathy, who was now nearing fifty and had matured in his ideas. But was Toussoun ready for mud brick? Not if he could help it. Residential Giza, after all, was not Middle Egypt. Nor did it resemble the once-fashionable district behind Abdin Palace where decades earlier the Abu Gabal family had resided in a European house of ninety rooms behind high stone gates and elegant French ironwork. Instead, Toussoun would insist that Fathy use the material the architect disliked the most: reinforced concrete.

Yet the dreamer's genius could not be so easily thwarted. Fathy devised a highly unconventional house for the time—one that was fresh, spirited, and spontaneous in its modernism, but also imbued with the memory of Islamic decoration. Fathy had flirted with the clean lines of the International Style in another rural home, and surely was familiar with the French architect Robert Mallet-Stevens and his cubistic Riviera villa that was the first modern house in France. At the same time, he continued to draw from his earlier studies of the ancient monuments of Cairo, a fact that greatly appealed to Toussoun, who administered a society for Islamic heritage founded by his grandfather.

Fathy conjured up more than a few surprises for Toussoun. The multilevel house's flat roofline gave little hint of a dome

The *salon arabe* in Hassan Fathy's hands has floor tiles of cement, inlays of blue glass, built-in banquettes, niches with lighting, copies of stained glass from the ruins of old houses, wrought-iron railing for a raised platform, to make one think that, as Ahmad Hamid declares, "he had a beat with modernity."

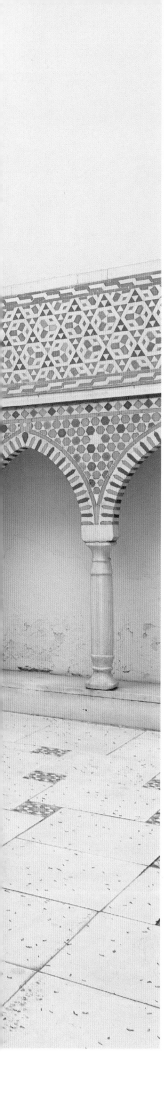

LEFT
Hassan Fathy reduced the staircase to "a service space . . . It never flows in a definite direction, which gives us more suspense. It is an unexplored space until landed," says architect Ahmad Hamid. Who indeed could have expected to find on the second floor, next to the bedrooms, a tiled open-air Moorish patio with a fountain?

RIGHT
"He demolished the lintel," says Hamid of a longitudinal door designed by Hassan Fathy to open into an enfilade of space; the Arabic inscription below the lunette is a saying of the Prophet and was imbedded into the wall "as if one material, as if it was earth to earth," the architect notes further.

rising up within. And who would have expected a colorful tiled patio with a fountain on the second floor? Or a front façade whose casual *mashrabiya* windows and stylized *muqaranas*, or suspended Moorish vaults, effectively suggested the mood that was to be found inside?

With its graceful, vaulted dome and arches, the main reception hall offered just the right atmosphere for a smattering of oriental windows in stained glass, inlaid wooden chairs, ceramic tiles, and lunettes embellished with Arabic inscriptions. Modern comforts included lights in the wall-niches and central air conditioning. And no matter how "poor" the materials—Fathy would use less marble, more wrought-iron, and modest floor tiles as well as light wooden paneling—every aspect was executed in high fashion. True to his cause, Fathy reversed the established Egyptian tendency to give priority to European décor. The Western styles were relegated to a side salon.

A master of space had arrived. Fathy created varying levels of steps and stairs connecting rooms that opened up harmoniously into one another like the rising and falling cadences of a symphony. Indeed, he would expand on the famous dictum that architecture is "frozen music," saying that it was "as if the eye sees one point after another to create a line of measurement [just as] one note leads into another to produce harmony and rhythm."

It was certainly more than Toussoun had dreamt of. With the addition of a concert grand piano for Toussoun's sister, who had studied at the Paris Conservatory, the Giza house soon became the site of weekly gatherings of family and friends, including Fathy himself, for musical recitals of both European and oriental pieces.

EL-MALLAWANY HOUSE

Near Tanta, province of Gharbiya. 1958–60

T he old black and white photographs looked almost new, despite seventy years of handling. At the center of one stood King Farouk, appearing even younger than his sixteen years, especially with his escort for nearly every occasion at his side, the craggy-faced Ali Pasha Maher. Greeting the new king that day in 1936 on his first official tour of the central Delta was his host, Ismail Bey El-Mallawany, heading a long line of local gentry decked out in high-cut collars and European jackets. Each also wore that unmistakable national emblem, the tarboosh.

A large landowner and a senator in parliament, Ismail Bey had received his guests in the front courtyard of his old family house. Even in a black and white photograph one could recognize in the background the festive red and blue muslin favored by Egyptians for celebrations ever since the pharaohs. The new king posed with Ismail Bey's oldest son Ibrahim, just out of law school in Paris, and his nephew, another Ibrahim, back from France where he had studied agriculture.

When Ismail Bey died four years later at age seventy-two, his passing marked the close of an era for his family, once Ottoman governors from Middle Egypt who had moved north to settle near the banks of the El-Kosed Canal. The main artery of the Nile to the east of Tanta had played as big a role in the family's farming of hundreds of *feddans*, as had his alliance to a clan of Delta landowners, the El-Menshawys. Ismail Bey had married the sister of a Menshawy; his son Ibrahim was later to wed the same man's daughter. It was "common practice to marry first cousins," explained Ibrahim's son, named Ismail after his grandfather, himself the product of that union of the two families known as the "little kings" of the central Delta cotton trade.

By the early 1950s Farouk had fallen from power, agricultural reform was coming, and Ismail Bey's wooden pavilion on the banks of the El-Kosed had disappeared. A widening of the "agricultural road" from Cairo to Alexandria had swept away just about everything, including the family's *gunayna*, or "garden," of two *feddans* worth of sycamores, figs, hedges, and green grass, and with marble *dikkas* offering welcoming seats along a vine-entwined arbor. Was this a "garden"? "We do not make a distinction in Arabic," the grandson, Ismail, explained, noting that for an Egyptian a "garden" could mean anything from a few flower beds to landscaped parks with pavilions. Gone too was Ismail Bey's old house, with its towers and wide porches, "good for roller-skating when I was a child," his grandson also recalled. The family's mosque on the road had remained untouched, as had an original side entrance gate.

Now Ibrahim asked a team of native Egyptian brothers to design him a "modern" country villa. He had been captivated by a rest house they had built called "The Ship," which he had seen on the corniche highway in Alexandria, just east of their new Automobile Club. Both structures featured a fresh, contemporary look and an exciting mixture of materials, including granite—to resist the vagaries of sea water—terracotta roof tiles, as well as bricks, imitation stone, handmade plaster, and concrete. Could these materials, which looked so well on the coastal corniche, also make heads turn on the agricultural road?

This was not to be a house only of reinforced concrete, for structural engineer Ahmed Khalil liked using a variety of materials to create a fluid modern look as well as offer practicality: he treated a projecting section at ground level with dressed stone to indicate that this was *madyafa*, or "public reception room."

197

As in most country houses in Egypt, a special room was assigned as the *salamlik*, or room for receiving guests, and here appropriately hangs the portrait of the house's builder, Mohamed Bey's son Ibrahim, wearing a tarboosh.

A baroque dining suite in ebony that was retained from the family's old house fits nicely into a modern room with built-in banquettes and, taking away the curve, a rectangular bow window.

OPPOSITE
"Mr. Cantilever," as the engineer Ahmed Khalil was known, added freestanding steps and a balcony to heighten the principal sitting room of a house he had built with his brother, Ali Sabet, a protégé of architect and professor Ali Labib Gabr.

Ibrahim wanted the Khalil brothers to do just that. Ali Sabet Khalil and his brother Ahmed—one an architect, the other a construction engineer—were known for their style and flair; and they were the only natives of Alexandria who could compete with the Italians, Greeks, and Swiss who dominated building in the Mediterranean port city.

The result was a playful villa with a front façade that glowed in the late afternoon sunset. One section was dressed in cut stone, putting a new twist on the old idea of the *madyafa*, or "reception office," where Ismail Bey had greeted his farm workers and constituents. To gaze over the top of the walls along the road was to discover an assortment of balconies, terraces, and overhangs—a delightful array of forms unique in the provinces.

Inside, Ismail Bey's bulky sofas and chairs might have been replaced, but his Italian baroque dining-room suite of rich, dark ebony now seemed refreshingly new against plain walls and a bay of rectangular windows. And why not have a free-floating set of stairs and balcony inside? These were signature designs for Ahmed Khalil, whose nickname was "Mr. Cantilever."

Would Ismail Bey himself have approved? Most likely. "He had great taste," his grandson recalled. "He liked to go to auction sales, looking for good bargains in furniture and objets d'art." His "town" house amid the olive groves of suburban Zeitoun was filled with French furniture, a salon Aubusson, and tapestries. "Between the wars," his grandson went on, "he went to central Europe with a Greek from Tanta to translate for him, and came back from Carlsbad with fine porcelains and Bohemian crystal glassware." He also had acquired "twelve overcoats, seventy-two suits, and a collection of canes."

There were no canes to be seen in the new villa, but there were a few dusty portraits of gentlemen in tarbooshes, an inlaid oriental chest or two, and low divans for the gallery and the sitting room at the top of the freestanding stairs. A portrait of the German emperor bought on an antiquing trip would leave a visiting French ambassador uneasy. But the old photographs of Farouk at home amused him greatly, before they went back into the drawer to await the next time they would be called up for a thoughtful but rapid remembrance of things past.

EL-MEZLAWY PALACE

Sohag, province of Sohag. 1950–60

T
o live over his factory did not seem out of the ordinary to Mohamed el-Mezlawy. "He was a practical man who liked his business," recalled his son Ibrahim. From his apartment he could oversee operations "twenty-four hours a day, seven days a week." If anything went wrong at night, all he had to do was jump out of bed, throw on his house robe, and dash downstairs to call a specialist. Once he had sent for such a man, but then, hoping for the best (*insha'allah*), he made some minor adjustments—and his cottonseed-oil press was up and running. Mohamed could sleep once more above the Great Sohag Factories, the largest in Upper Egypt.

In the 1940s the oil press also produced margarine, kitchen soap, even ice, a necessity more than a luxury in the Upper Egyptian summer. Moreover, Mohamed had flour mills, warehouses, laboratories for testing products, and a service center for ironworks. His German-made electric power station was the first of its kind in Egypt, and the first to use buried cables and underground terminals. It produced, according to Ibrahim, "enough power to light the entire city of Sohag."

Mohamed had absorbed a passion for machinery from his uncle and father-in-law, Ahmed Khalil. In 1895, Khalil had invented Egypt's first water pump, and for the first time, everyone had pure, fresh drinking water. The family had come a long way since the 1880s, when they set up a wheat-grinding business in El-Mazlawa, just south of the provincial capital of Sohag. It was nearly a century since the family's founder had arrived "by camel carrying his pieces of gold," as Ibrahim described the merchant Abd el-Kadir, who had moved south from the Delta because of poor health.

Mohamed could neither read nor write, but "he knew technical things perfectly, and always had a new idea," according to his son. He expanded his uncle's water-drilling business, and with his brother ran a purchasing office in Cairo's iron-market district. The language of the trade was French, and Mohamed had "a teacher who came by each day to give him lessons," said his son. "French became our second language, but later on we switched to English."

No sooner had Mohamed returned to Sohag to build his factory and open eighteen supply branches as far south as the Sudanese border than he had another idea. He fenced in his factory, leaving only the northern side open. "I'm expanding," he announced. "Where?" everyone wanted to know. "Cairo," he proclaimed. But his intentions were in Sohag. There on the west bank of the Nile he would build a palace worthy of the capital.

Mohamed did not intend to live in his palace, however. "He built it for the joy of it," declared Ibrahim. "He wanted something beautiful he could be proud of." The local architect and engineer who designed the factory, Abd el-Meniem Araman, was kept busy each afternoon for ten years with Mohamed's "white revenge." As his son explained, "My father refused all color, even for his factory." The only exception was his 1958 Mercury, in black and white with polished nickel fittings.

The discovery of a ruined Ottoman mosque in the Delta gave Mohamed the idea for a white marble palace. Having had

OPPOSITE
With the family quarters above, the entire ground level is devoted to a hall that rises up to an upper gallery and skylight and creates a grandiose space for great public receptions that is befitting an Egyptian palace.

OVERLEAF LEFT
Mixed materials of concrete, ceramics, and brick bring a modern feeling to the El-Mezlawy Palace, which was inspired by the styles of Andalusian Spain.

OVERLEAF RIGHT
An inscription on a column of the Sohag palace assures guests, in Arabic, that this is the house of the El-Mezlawys.

its stones refurbished in Cairo, he reused them both inside and outside of his new palace. From Mansoura, the eastern Delta city famed for its Italian craftsmen, came sixty artisans, who fitted the huge pieces of marble together. Mohamed "invented the decoration" himself, his son confirmed.

Inside, the enormous reception hall of high Moorish arches met with arabesques, calligraphy, and geometric designs. Against the walls were fine, oversized cabinets of oriental marquetry purchased from the Nasser government's disposal of Prince Mohamed Ali Tewfik's estates—including one in Nag Hammadi, where the prince had created a showplace of Islamic art and architecture to rival his Manial Palace in Cairo. "My father bought an entire lot," Ibrahim noted.

A huge chandelier had once hung in the Abdin Palace. The wooden Art Nouveau–style cabinets were the work of François Linke, the Bohemian craftsman whose Paris workshops had found a client in King Fuad in the 1920s. Mohamed had "stored the furniture for many years before placing it in the center hall," his son recalled.

Not until 1960 would Mohamed finally move into his Andalusian sensation. His factory would be nationalized shortly afterward. After permitting the governor of Sohag to use his palace to receive visiting parliamentarians of the United Arab Republic of Egypt and Syria, Mohamed came up with yet another idea. By then in his early sixties, he envisioned turning his palace into a local public showplace, dredging out a harbor in the Nile "deep enough even for cruise ships," reported his son Ibrahim.

BIBLIOGRAPHY

Abd al-Nur, Fakhry. *Memoirs*. Naguib Greis, translator. Cairo: Dar al-Shiruq, 1992.

Alexandria 1860–1960, Alexandria: Harpocrates Publishing, 1997.

Alexandria entre deux mondes. Aix-en-Provence: Editions Edisud, n.d.

Al-Rafii, Abd al-Rahman. *Asr Ismail*. 2 vols. Second edition. Cairo: 1948.

Balboni, L.A. *Gli Italiani nella Civitá Egiziana del Secolo XIX*. 2 vols. Alexandria: Societá Dante Alighieri, 1906.

Ball, Warwick. *Syria, A Historical and Architectural Guide*. London: Melisende, 1997.

Barillari, Diana, and Godoli, Ezio. *Istanbul 1900, Art Nouveau Architecture and Interiors*. Italy: Octavo Press, 1996.

Berque, Jacques. *Imperialism and Revolution*. New York: 1972.

Boutros Ghali, Mirrit. *Mémoires de Nubar Pacha*. Beirut: Librairie du Liban, 1983.

Bulletin de la Sociéte Archéologique d'Alexandrie, No. 2. Alexandria, 1899.

Caillard, Mabel. *A Lifetime in Egypt, 1876–1935*. London: Grant Richard, 1935.

Chennels, Ellen. *Recollections of an Egyptian Princess*. 2 vols. London: William Blackwood and Sons, 1893.

Crosnier Leconte, Marie-Laure, and Volait, Mercédès, *L'Egypte d'un Architecte Ambroise Baudry, 1838–1906*, Paris: Somogy, Editions d'Art, 1998.

De Guerville, A.B. *New Egypt*. London: William Heinemann, 1905.

De Leon, Edwin. *The Khedive's Egypt*. New York: Harper and Brothers, 1878.

Delchevalérie, G. *Flore Exotique de Jardin D'Acclimation de Ghezireh et des Domains de S. A. Le Khedive*. Cairo: 1871.

———. *Les Promenades et les Jardins du Caire*. Charmes, 1899

Djavidan Hanum, Prinzessin. *Harem*. Berlin: Verlag für Kulturpolitik, 1930.

Douin, G. *Histoire du Regne du Khedive Ismail. Tome II, L'Apogée 1867–1873*. Cairo: La Reale Societá di Geografia d'Egitto, 1934.

Forster, E. M. *Alexandria: A History and A Guide*. London: Michael Haag Ltd., 1986.

Goldschmidt, Arthur, Jr., *Biographical Dictionary of Modern Egypt*. Cairo: The American University in Cairo Press, 2000.

Goodwin, Godfrey. *A History of Ottoman Architecture*. London: Thames and Hudson, 1971.

Hassan, Hassan. *In the House of Muhammad Ali: A Family Album, 1805–1952*. Cairo: The American University in Cairo Press, 2000.

Hunter, Robert F. *Egypt under the Khedives*. Pittsburg: University of Pittsburg Press, 1984.

Ilbert, Robert. *Alexandrie 1830–1930*. Cairo: Institut Français d'Archéologie Orientale (IFAO), 1996.

James, T.G.H. *Howard Carter: The Path to Tutankhamun*. Cairo: The American University in Cairo Press, 2001.

Lane-Poole, Stanley. *The Art of the Saracens in Egypt*. Facsimile edition. London: Darf Publishers, Ltd., 1993.

Loti, Pierre. *Egypt*. London: T. Werner Laurie, Ltd., 1908.

Luthi, Jean-Jacques. *L'Egypte des Rois 1922–1953*. Paris: L'Harmattan, 1997.

———. *La Vie Quotidienne en Egypt au Temps des Khedives 1863–1914*. Paris: L'Harmattan, 1998.

Lyster, William. *The Citadel of Cairo*. Cairo: The Palm Press, 1993.

Mamluk Art, the Splendour and Magic of the Sultans. Cairo: Museum With No Frontiers, Al-Dar Al-Masriah Al-Lubnaniah, 2001.

Marsot, Afaf Lutfi Al-Sayyid. *Egypt in the Reign of Muhammad Ali*. Cambridge: 1984.

Mazel, Jean. *Le Sucre en Egypte*. Cairo: E. & R. Schindler, 1937.

Mubarak, Ali. *Al-Khitat al-Tawfiqiyya al-Jadida*. 20 vols. Cairo: 1886–87.

Murray, G.W. *Sons of Ishmael: A Story of the Egyptian Bedouin*. London: 1935.

Nelson, Nina. *The Mena House Oberoi*. Cairo: The Palm Press, 1997.

Österreich und Ägypten, Cairo: Osterreichisches Kulturinstitut Kairo, 1993.

Politis, Athanase G. *L'Hellenisme et L'Egypte Moderne*. 2 vols. Paris: Librairie Felix Alcan. 1928.

Prisse d'Avennes, E. *Islamic Art in Cairo*. Cairo: The American University in Cairo Press, 1999.

Raafat, Samir W. *Maadi, 1904–1962. Society and History in a Cairo Suburb*. Cairo: The Palm Press, 1995.

———. *Cairo, The Glory Years*. Alexandria: Harpocrates Publishing, 2003.

Ramleh, als Winteraufenthalt, Leipzig: Woerl's Reisebucher-Verlag, 1900.

Raymond, André. *Le Caire vu par Pascal Coste 1817–1827*, Cairo, 2001.

Reid, Donald M. *Whose Pharaohs–* Berkeley: University of California Press, 2002.

Sakr, Tarek Mohamed Refaat. *Early Twentieth-Century Islamic Architecture in Cairo*. Cairo: The American University in Cairo Press, 1992.

Sammarco, Angelo. *Gli Italiani in Egitto*. Alexandria: Edizioni Del Fascio, 1937.

Sonbol, Amira El-Azhary. *Mémoires d'un souverain par Abbas Helmi, Khedive d'Egypte*, Cairo: Recherches et Témoignages, CNRS, 1996.

Steele, James. *An Architecture For People: The Complete Works of Hassan Fathy*. Cairo: The American University in Cairo Press, 1997.

Storrs, Ronald. *Orientations*. London: Nicholson & Watson, 1937.

Tamraz, Nihal, *Nineteenth-Century Cairene Houses and Palaces*. Cairo: The American University in Cairo Press, 1998.

Toussaint, Yvon. *Les Barons Empain*. Librairie Artheme Fayard, 1996.

Tugay, Emine Foat. *Three Centuries, Family Chronicles of Turkey and Egypt*. London: Oxford University Press, 1963.

Volait, Mercédès. *L'Architecture Moderne en Egypte et La Revue Al-'Imara 1939–1959*. Cairo: Centre d'Etudes et de Documentation Economique, Juridique et Sociale (CEDEJ), 1998.

———. *Le Caire-Alexandrie, Architectures européennes 1850–1950*. Cairo: Centre d'Etudes et de Documentation Economique, Juridique et Sociale (CEDEJ), Institut Français d'Archéologie Orientale (IFAO), 2001.

Wiese, André B. *Aus dem Gastebuch des Winter Palace in Luxor (1920-1935), Ein aegyptisches Glasperlenspiel*. Berlin: Gebr. Mann Verlag, 1998.

Wiet, Gaston. *Mohamed Ali et les Beaux-Arts*. Cairo: ca. 1949.

William II (formerly Kaiser Wilhelm II of Germany). *My Memoirs: 1878–1918*. London: Cassell and Co., Ltd., 1922.

Williams, Caroline. *Islamic Monuments in Cairo*. Cairo: The American University in Cairo Press, 2002.

Wissa, H. F. *Assiout: the Saga of an Egyptian Family*. Sussex: The Book Guild, Ltd., 1994.

Wright, Arnold. *Twentieth Century Impressions of Egypt*. London: Lloyd's Greater Britain Publishing Co., Ltd., 1909.

"Yussuf Kemal," *Egypte Aujourd'hui* 27 (1995).

INDEX

EDITOR: Elaine M. Stainton
DESIGNER: Darilyn Lowe Carnes
PRODUCTION MANAGER: Jane G. Searle

Library of Congress Cataloging-in-Publication Data
Johnston, Shirley.
Egyptian palaces and villas : pashas, khedives, and kings / by Shirley Johnston, with Sherif
Sonbol.
    p. cm.
Includes bibliographical references and index.
ISBN 0–8109–5538–5 (hardcover : alk. paper)
1. Palaces—Egypt. 2. Country homes—Egypt. 3. Architecture—Egypt—19th century.
4. Architecture—Egypt—20th century.   I. Sunbul, Sharīf. II. Title.
NA1581.J64 2006
728.80962'09034_dc22

                                2005026817

BINDING CASE: The painted and gilded stucco ceiling of the Blue Salon in the Manial Palace

ENDPAPERS: One of two white marble plaques listing the artisans who worked on the
carpentry, marble, and stone work for the mosque at the Manial Palace, including the great
master of calligraphy, Ahmed Kamil Effendi

Photographs © 2000–2005 by Shirley Johnston and Sherif Sonbol
Copyright © 2006 Shirley Johnston

Published in 2006 by Abrams, an imprint of Harry N. Abrams, Inc.
All rights reserved. No portion of this book may be reproduced, stored in a retrieval system,
or transmitted in any form or by any means, mechanical, electronic, photocopying,
recording, or otherwise, without written permission from the publisher.

Printed and bound in China
10 9 8 7 6 5 4 3 2 1

HNA
harry n. abrams, inc.
a subsidiary of La Martinière Groupe

115 West 18th Street
New York, NY 10011
www.hnabooks.com

الكتابة خط
الحاج أحمد كامل أفندى
الحاج أحمد كامل أفندى
الخطاط الطبيب
باستانبول

النجارة والسقف
النجارين المعلم
محمد إبراهيم النجار

السلام من عمل
المعلم محمد إبراهيم
طلحة

الرخام من عمل
المعلم السقاء
ومحمود صالح

الحمل من عمل
المعلم محمد غلفى
الخطاط

القيشانى
صنع فى
استانبول

البناء من عمل
المعلم أحمد محمود
البنا وأولاده

ملاحظ هذا
لأعمال سيادة اللواء
متولى باشا وكيل الدائرة

تمت هذه
الأعمال بفضل
الله العظيم